From the Bottom of the Pile

An exploration of a family history

by Brian Dowden

To Simon,

Many thanks for all your help

Brian

First published November 2011

Published by B. E. & S. J. Dowden.
Woodbridge, Suffolk, England.

ISBN 978-0-9570821-0-6.

Typeset in Perpetua and printed and bound by Gipping Press Ltd.,
Unit 2, Lion Barn Estate, Needham Market, Suffolk, IP6 8NZ.
T: 01449 721599 • www.gippingpress.co.uk

© Brian E. Dowden.

All rights reserved. No part of this publication may be reproduced, stored in a retrieval system, or transmitted in any form or by any means, electronic, mechanical, photocopying, recorded or otherwise, without the prior permission of the publisher.

Contents

Preface	i
Introduction	iii
Social and Religious Background	1
Earliest recorded Forebears to mid-18th century	13
Thomas and Mary	21
Ralph and Families	27
William and Mary	35
Enclosure; and James	41
Charles, Ellen and their Children	45
Joseph, Jessie and their Children	55
Dad, with Mum and Family	65
Appendix	85
Ancestral Documents	89
Family Trees	111

Preface

The essays in this document were written by Brian E. Dowden, born 8th October 1933, and they are mainly addressed to my direct descendants. In common with many people I had no interest in family history during my younger years. Perhaps the young man is properly more concerned with his possible future rather than with his family's past. However we are not forever young, and in my early 50's I began to take an interest in my father's family tree. However there was a problem; my father had died some 15 years previously, and in any event he had been orphaned at just five years of age. Also I was not in contact with any other member of my father's family. The only information on which to base my ancestral investigation was that my father's father lived in Pimlico, and was a foreman chimney sweep named Joseph who died some three months after his wife Jessie in 1907. My father also stated, with great bitterness, that Joseph died of a broken heart following the death of Jessie. I also recalled an Uncle Mick who was my father's elder brother, but I received no family history information from that source.

Initially my investigation work was carried out on a sporadic basis, but then one day in the mid-1990's a breakthrough was made. Joseph Dowden's father was Charles, and Charles spent his life in the hamlet of Heathrow which was adjacent to the village of Harmondsworth, Middlesex. The sporadic investigation then became a regular activity. The following essays record the information found during the family history search.

Writing now after 15+ years of investigation into the lives of my paternal forebears I place on record my appreciation of, and thanks to, my wife Sheila. Without her active encouragement and support during this long period of time, my peering into my family's history would not have been possible.

Copyright

Genealogy is an activity in which many members of a given family may be interested. It is therefore not desirable, or indeed legal, for information that can be found in original historical records to be owned by an individual researcher under the laws of copyright.

However the following information on my forebears has been obtained as a consequence of searching through a large number of original documents held in diverse locations. The searching process necessarily included the examination of documents indicating the absence of ancestral records in addition to the finding of relevant family-related papers. It was only after the collation of many family-related papers, obtained from disparate sources, that the production of this family history was possible. Thus the document From the Bottom of the Pile is subject to copyright and all rights are reserved by the author.

From the Bottom of the Pile

Introduction

Obviously we each have two parents, four grandparents and so on. Thus a genealogical investigation involving (say) eight generations can mean the tracing of 256+128+ ---- 4 + 2 = 510 direct forebears. Clearly this is an immense task and hence I began the investigation by concentrating only on 'Dowden' forebears, and this took me back to a man who was born in about the year 1700. However a fragment of paper written on 25th April 1726, after a Court Baron in Harmondsworth, gave the maiden name of the wife of my '1700' grandfather. By investigating her family tree, my ancestors are now traced back to a man who was born in about the year 1600.

As I spent many hours, in various locations, searching through and then collating various church, manorial, state and privately owned documents, some of the events that occurred in my forebears lives became apparent. Then, as these events were discovered, I found myself feeling that I was developing an actual acquaintance with the people whose lives were being partially revealed. Of course one cannot 'know' one's ancestors; two-way communication is impossible and hence one cannot deduce their attitudes towards such things as living environment, patterns of work and so on. However the legal framework and local conditions in which our ancestors led their lives can be determined, and I believe that an understanding of their circumstances adds significantly to the story. For this reason the first essay in this work is concerned with the social and religious background that applied in the home area of my forebears. The second essay notes the local rules relevant to the Manor of Harmondsworth until 1819. From these the reader will see that the day-to-day regulations governing my forebears lives were very different from those of today.

In deducing one's family tree several factors quickly become apparent. As one investigates further back in time, relevant records become fewer in number and further tracing eventually becomes impracticable, if not indeed impossible. For 18th century and earlier records there is no consistency in spelling. This applies especially to the writing of surnames by a clerk when the person stating his or her surname could not read or write. Then also people were 'careless' about certain facts. For example in the census records from 1841 to 1881 my great-grandfather is recorded, but in none of these five records was the second digit of his age noted as the same number.

Despite all the problems concerning the records of past events it is beyond reasonable doubt that the story of my identified ancestors begins in the early 17th century. The location is the Parish and Manor of Harmondsworth, Middlesex, a village some 18 miles west of London. The ancestors in question were neither vagrants nor significant land-owners. They relied on manual labour for their livelihoods and they were -- by any meaningful definition-- poor. In short, they were 'from the bottom of the pile'.

From the Bottom of the Pile

Social and Religious Background

We all have a family history that is eventually lost in the mists of time, and for me this fog relates to events before about the year 1600. Also my earliest known ancestor spent at least a part of his life in the parish and manor of Harmondsworth, Middlesex. However the social situations of this man, and those that followed him in Stuart and Hanoverian Harmondsworth were a consequence of earlier events; and hence the following account starts with an overview of earlier times common to most of southern England.

If we look at the structure of early medieval society the kings were at the top of the social scale, with the church also playing a prominent role. In return for certain defined services, land was 'owned' by persons or organisations appointed by the king, and the manor comprised the lowest level of such ownership. The general populace or villeins, comprising agricultural labourers and skilled workers such as blacksmiths, were bound to the land in their manor, and they were obliged to spend part of their time working for the benefit of their Lord of the Manor. This was not however an arrangement in which the villein earned a living wage, the subsistence level of the villein's life was procured by his cultivating a small part of the manorial land (say about four acres) for the benefit of himself and his family. The villein also had the right to take wood for cooking etc. from waste land, to graze a small number of livestock animals on the common pastures, and to take hay from the common meadow. From the above the villein's life could seem idyllic, but starvation conditions were common, and the Lord of the Manor always required his agricultural needs to be met at the very time the villein needed to work on his own land. In Norman times the extent of a villein's land holding was subject to the pleasure of the Lord of the Manor, however during Plantagenet times it became custom, and eventually practice, for a deceased villein's area of land to be inherited according to the villein's Will as generation succeeded generation. However, in the final analysis, it was always the Lord of the Manor who owned the title to the land.

Also at this time, and for centuries to come in Harmondsworth, the farming system was 'open field'. This system was introduced during Saxon times and was one in which a farming area had three large areas or fields, each of many acres. Two of these areas were cultivated in any given year and the third was left fallow. In each area the fields were divided into long narrow strips and any one individual in the manor would occupy (i.e. cultivate) separate areas of land in a range of these strips. This prevented the bunching of land into one holding and hence the occupancy of the best land by any one individual. The fields were not fenced or hedged, and strips were ploughed in a manner such that each strip became a ridge with furrows on either side to act as drains.

After the Black Death in the mid-fourteenth century the villein broke free from total bondage to the land, and money began to play a role in his life. Thus as the fourteenth century faded into the fifteenth, with the eventual establishment of the Tudor dynasty, the land holding of a villein

From the Bottom of the Pile

became an occupation by right, called villeinagium, and it was recognised by law. Transfer of land to succeeding generations or to third parties was confirmed by a legally constituted assembly known as a Court Baron. This court acted on behalf of the Lord of the Manor and it comprised the 'Steward' of the manor and a small jury of the more substantial tenants in the manor (i.e. men who occupied or had legal title (under the Lord of the Manor) to substantial housing and areas of land). The Steward was the chief agent for the Lord for the management of his Manor, and in Harmondsworth (as was usual elsewhere) he presided over the Court Baron and employed a clerk who kept the records. The court jury was referred to as 'The Homage', a term that derived from the ceremonial pledges of loyalty and obligation owed by tenants to their lord. All decisions of a Court Baron were recorded on a sheet of parchment -- i.e. a prepared sheet of sheep or goat skin -- and the completed parchment was then formed into a tight roll for storage. A roll of Court Baron parchment was known as a 'copy-roll' and hence occupation of land under the above system was known as a copyhold tenancy. On transfer of copyhold land the new tenant had to swear fealty to the Lord of the Manor and to pay a 'heriot' or fine to the court. In early times this may have been the new tenant's best cow or pig, but by Tudor times the fine was both imposed and paid in cash. This cash, less the expenses incurred by the Steward in constituting the Court, was paid to the Lord of the Manor and it formed part of his income. In practice a tenant could die at any time of year and, at least in Harmondsworth, a Court Baron was a once-yearly occurrence. During the period between the death of a tenant and the next Court Baron the copyhold land of the deceased would be held by one of the more substantial members of the manor on behalf of the Lord. It was only at the next meeting of a Court Baron that land previously belonging to a deceased person would be passed to his/her beneficiaries.

The Lordship of the Manor of Harmondsworth was held by King Harold before his death at the Battle of Hastings. After the battle, King William acquired the Lordship of the Manor and in due course the Lordship was passed to the Abbey of the Holy Trinity, Rouen, France. But medieval England was often at war with France and thus French institutions, with manors in England, progressively saw these holdings confiscated by the English Crown. This happened at Harmondsworth in 1391 when the lordship of the manor was confiscated from the abbey at Rouen and awarded to William Wykeham, Bishop of Winchester, as part of the endowment of Winchester College. Incidentally the Great Barn at Harmondsworth was built in the 1400's in order to store grain for use at Winchester. This barn, still in existence today, is of cathedral-like proportions and my ancestors, over a period of some 250 years, must have spent many hours within its confines threshing, storing and removing for use successive crops of corn. During the 1400's there occurred the Wars of the Roses, and during this time a number of previously obscure families rose to become citizens of substance. Many of these families continued to prosper during the Tudor dynasty, and one such was the Paget family. In 1546 William Paget was awarded the Lordship of the Manor of West Drayton and this was followed during the next year with the award of the Manor of Harmondsworth. With a short gap, important in terms of my family history, the Paget family retained the lordship of the Manor of Harmondsworth until it was sold in the early 19th century. By this time the title had no worthwhile value.

Social and Religious Background

Returning now to the medieval period, church-based manors were (often) credited as acting charitably towards those of the poor who could not maintain themselves. Then later, as religious foundations lost their manorial holdings to a new class of 'men of substance', the number of religious sources of charity for the poor were reduced. Also, progressively during this period, poverty was seen as a condition ordained by God and hence not worthy of charity born out of religious zeal. It followed that because any form of locally based relief for the poor was not obligatory by law, it was limited to that necessary for the maintenance of law and order in an England yet to develop a standing army or police force. Following the Wars of the Roses, groups of ex-military personnel formed themselves into bands of sturdy beggars that threatened neighbourhoods, and these bands, once formed, continued well into the reign of King Henry VIII. Action became necessary in three areas, viz. laws to discourage vagrancy, schemes to provide work for the able poor, and systems of relief for the poor who were unable to support themselves. With regard to the incapable poor, systems of relief based on local rate charges were established in the mid-16th century and then, at the end of the 16th century a range of Poor Laws were enacted by national legislation. My known forebears were much affected by these laws.

The first 'Act for the Relief of the Poor' is dated 1597-8. It embodied many of the earlier practices that were operated locally, but it also required the appointment of an overseer in every parish. The overseer had the duty to provide for those of the poor who had no means to maintain themselves. Overseers were also required to submit a full account of their activities and finances to two justices at the end of each year, (i.e. the 25th March at this time). These justices, being local, had an interest in minimising rate charges, and to this end the overseer was given considerable authority over the lives of ordinary subjects. The 1597-8 Act was superseded by a further Act in 1601, and it was the fundamental structure of the 1601 Act that impacted on the lives of the poor until the mid-1830's.

In the 1601 Act, parishes were required 'to relieve the lame, impotent, old, blind etc. being poor and unable to work'. Assessments for the Poor Rate were made by the churchwardens and the overseer. These assessments were first based on the area of land occupied and then later on its rental value. The poor (liable to be in receipt of benefit) could be excused from the payment of rates. Indolence was not an option for the able poor. Under the 1601 Act employment was generated via a requirement for overseers to purchase materials on which the able poor were able to work in exchange for relief. Also, a parish's churchwardens and the overseer were empowered to bind any child from the age of seven years, whose parents they judge to be unable to support them, to be apprentices where they think fit, until a male child attains 24 years of age and a female child attains 20 years of age or on her marriage. There are known records of two Dowden children being 'sent away' under Poor Law legislation in the early part of the 19th century.

The 1601 Act was passed when the majority of the population of about 3 millions was engaged in agriculture, and when the parish was the most important unit in a social structure designed to meet the needs of self-sufficient rural communities. At this time the towns were small enough for their parish structures to operate as above. Indeed, as if to emphasize the rural nature of the country, the 1601 Act required that new workers cottages were to include access to four acres of land for the cottage tenants use. Unfortunately the late Elizabethan was unable to forecast the changes that were to occur in Stuart and Hanoverian England. From the 1660 restoration on, trade was increasing to a significant degree, and with this development people were not tied to their parish to the same extent as hitherto. However despite a growing need for mobility, parish 'A' was not prepared to support the needy poor from parish 'B'. This led to the 1662 Act 'For the Better Relief of the Poor'. This Act made each parish responsible for the upkeep of only its own poor, and empowered the parish to evict an immigrant within 40 days of his arrival unless he was able to rent a property of at least £10-00 a year in value. After a 1692 amendment, the qualifications for settlement were: by serving a whole year in a parish office; by paying local rates; by hiring and service; by apprenticeship; or by inheritance from one's father. This Act not only enabled a parish forcibly to remove 'unqualified immigrants' but had side effects that became common practice. For example, a man and his wife in parish 'A' have children, and the husband dies while the children are still young. If the widow later married a man from parish 'B' she would gain parish 'B' settlement rights, however her children would still be 'settled in parish 'A'. If the children then became a burden on parish 'B' they would be subject to the full rigours of the Poor Laws.

If an adult left his/her place of settlement in order to find employment, but was unsuccessful in meeting the Poor Law criteria the consequences were severe. The unfortunate person could expect the new place of abode to bring about a conviction for vagrancy as soon as he/she was no longer self-sufficient. This in its turn resulted in a period in the House of Correction (a very unpleasant prospect) and also to being stripped to the waist (male and female) and having one's back whipped until it was raw and bloody. Return to the 'vagrants' place of settlement was then forcibly carried out by a network of agents who made such activity their business. Further to the above, in order to meet the obligation to find employment for the able poor, in the late 17th century some groups of parishes, called 'Unions', took out private Parliamentary Bills to set up joint workhouses. An Act of 1723 then allowed individual parishes to establish a workhouse and to withhold relief from anyone refusing to enter it. This Act also allowed 'farming out' the maintenance of the poor to a contractor for a fixed rate per head. My own 4*great grandfather was born in parish 'A', and was married in parish 'B' in 1725 to my 4*great grandmother who was born and settled in parish 'C'. They also wished to live and raise their children in parish 'C'. How they complied with the Poor Law criteria in parish 'C' is noted in the essay concerning my earliest forebears.

While the above civil laws concerning the poor were being developed in England there were also significant changes in religious practice. In mainland Europe the reformation occurred, with resulting religious conflict for many years. To a large extent England became a Protestant country and it allowed the immigration of Europeans whose religious beliefs were not accepted by their Roman Catholic rulers. These immigrants from mainland Europe were registered and

Social and Religious Background

referred to as 'strangers', i.e. foreigners. Also, perhaps despite not being 'Church of England', they were allowed to establish their own churches in places such as London. The Huguenots from France were one such group of immigrants to England during the mid to late 16th century and also during the late 17th century. Another, less well known group came from Wallonia (in present day Belgium) during the late 16th century. It is perhaps a Wallonian 'stranger' who is my earliest known ancestor.

The next essay concerns those manorial rules For Harmondsworth that remain in the (discovered) public record. To understand fully the circumstances in which my Harmondsworth forebears led their lives the reader is invited, at the very least, to peruse these papers.

From the Bottom of the Pile

Manorial Rules of Life

In the 21st. century we do not question the interdependence of members of society for the materials and services we depend upon for life. Towns import all required food etc. from elsewhere, and in earlier times this type of existence did not occur. The vast majority of the population lived in small villages, and even the towns were no more than large villages in the countryside. The villages were contained in Manors, and each manor was, in essence, an independent entity in that it produced all the goods and services necessary for life. The land (and in medieval times also most of the peasants) were owned by a Lord of the Manor, and he decided the rules within which the population in his manor must live. Of course certain rules were nationally set and 'murder' is an obvious example, but within the national framework, rules were local and had the force of law. As England moved from the medieval period, a system of Court's Baron was established and these were used to enact the transfer of land within a manor. A Court Baron operated under the Chairmanship of a lawyer referred to as the Steward acting on behalf of the Lord of the Manor, with other prominent citizens within the manor acting at the behest of the Steward and being known as 'The Homage'. The term 'homage' being a reference to the fact that these citizens (like all others) owed feudal allegiance to the Lord of the Manor. For the Manor of Harmondsworth some of the local rules survive, and these are noted below.

Before noting sets of rules the reader is reminded of the farming system in operation from Saxon times until (mostly) the end of the 18th century. Within each manor there existed a relatively low number of large, unfenced fields. Each field was divided into a number of strips and each strip was separately ploughed. This led to a ridged land structure with drainage occurring on each side of a strip. A given landowner would then be the tenant of given lengths of strips from different fields so that no one man would have control over an area containing the best land. Ownership of land within a manor was by a 'copyhold' arrangement, that is the freehold of all land belonged to the lord of the manor, and all manorial subjects technically rented their parcels of land from the lord. By Tudor times the occupier of a parcel of land could sell or bequeath his area to whomsoever he chose providing he paid a fee (known as a heriot or fine) to his lord of the manor. The new occupier then had the same rights as his predecessor. Transfer of land could only take place at a Court Baron. In this arrangement of land management there were significant areas of common land from which manorial occupiers could keep a goat etc. and cut brushwood for cooking and so on.

The earliest example of local rules for the Manor of Harmondsworth seen by the writer are dated 1651. The document states:

'It is ordered that no person shall bait any horse or cow upon any mans land except his own or in the common field, And if any person break the order aforesaid he shall forfeit 5s-0d. Also it is ordered that no sheep shall roam into the stubble within the common field until the 8th day of September next ------?------, and for every ????? (stock?) that shall offend shall forfeit 1s-0d. And it is ordered to 'hand for staking days'

From the Bottom of the Pile

at the foreman's appointment and if any Juryman fails he shall forfeit ------ (illegible).

It is agreed that John Tillear, ?? Watts, Christopher Atlee and James Sheffield shall act as overseers to the Jury for staking.

The above document is not complete, but it does give a flavour of aspects of local control.

Moving forward 120+ years there are three surviving documents which now are noted below. Notice that the title of the first paper appears to be very democratic, but in practice attendance at this meeting was limited to only the local men of influence.

General meeting of inhabitants in the parish of Harmondsworth
26th September 1774

At a general meeting of the Churchwardens and Overseers of the Parish of Harmondsworth in the County of Middlesex and other (of) the Inhabitants of the said Parish having a right to afsemble in Vestry or other Public Meetings for transacting the Businefs of the said Parish the twentysixth day of September in the year of our Lord One thousand and seven hundred and seventyfour.

1st.   That a workhouse be erected ------

2nd.   In order to pay the charges and expenses to attend the erecting ---- four hundred pounds -----.

Then, various other agreements regarding the workhouse master and mistress, the impact on the Poor Rate etc. The document was then signed by some twelve of the prominent tenants in the parish.

Five years after the above General Meeting, the Homage issued a statement that was, in effect, the law of the Manor of Harmondsworth until the passing of the Enclosure Act in 1814. The statement is repeated in full below, with original spelling and use of upper case letters.

Manor of Harmondsworth in the County of Middlesex

The Presentiments of the Homage at the Court Baron held for said Manor on Thursday the Twenty second day of July 1779

First we find and Present that all Copyhold Messuages Lands and Tenements within the said Manor are Copyhold of Inheritance and are held of the lord within the said Manor by yearly rents suits of Court fealtys and other services therefor due

Also we find and Present that upon the death of any Tenant dying Seized of Any Ancient Copyhold Messuage or Messuages of Inheritance in the said Manor a Heriot Custom was and is by Custom of the said Manor due to the Lord

Also we find and Present that by the custom of the said Manor Every Copyhold Tenant of any Messuage Cottage Lands or Tenements of the said Manor might and may at his Will and Pleasure without Licence from the Lord Lawfully Sell cut down or grub up any Timber trees or Other trees or Wood Standing or Growing on his Lands or Premises and might and may also without any Licence Sell Burn or Dispose of the same at his or their Will and Pleasure

8

Manorial Rules of Life

Also we find and Present that by the custom of the said Manor Every Copyhold Tenant of Inheritance within the said Manor might and may without Licence from the Lord thereof take or Pull down or cause to be taken or Pulled down any of his or their Respective Copyhold Messuage or Cottage or Tenement Barns Stables or other Outhouses or Buildings Whatsoever And may permit and suffer the same so to Remain unbuilt and may at his or their Will and Pleasure without Licence Build the Same or may Erect or New build on the same Lands and Premises or any other (of) their Respective Lands and Tenements within the said Manor any Messuages Cottages Barnes Stables or other house or Building Whatsoever saving the Statute in that Behalf

Also we find and Present that by the Custom of said Manor every Copyhold Tenant may make a lease or Leases Demise or Demises of any Copyhold Messuage Cottage Lands or Tenements within the said Manor for the term of three Years or Under without Licence of or from the Land thereof Saving to the Lord of the Manor his Rents and Services

Also we find and Present that every Inhabitant within the said Manor being a Householder or Master of a family hath an Ancient Custom time out of Mind used and had a liberty of fishing In the Comon River or Rivers within the said Manor by three days in the Week that is to Say Wednesdays Fridays and Satterdays

Also we find and Present that by the Custom of the said Manor no other Tenant of the said Manor but only Messuage holders to take any Surrender or Surrenders or Serve on the Homage which Messuage Holders are such Tenants who hold by Copy of Court Roll of the said Manor one or more Messuage or Messuages

Also we find and Present that the Lords of said Manor have time out of Mind and as often as occation hath required at their own proper Costs and Charges Builded Repaired and Amended and so Ought to build repair and Amend the footbridges called Moorbridge Middlebridge and Hawthorn Bridge going over the Rivers in the Comon moor within the said Manor and have always found Timber and other Materials for the Same

Also we find and Present that every Freeholder and Copyholder within the said Manor have time out of mind had and so Claim to have Liberty without Licence from the Lord of the said Manor to Drag and take Earth called Moor Earth out of the Rivers Lakes and Brooks within the Wastes of the said Manor for the Better dressing and Manuring of their Lands and Grounds within the said Manor and no moor earth to be sold to any out Parishioners on the Penalty of five Shillings a Load And also if any Inhabitant of the said Parish carry any moor earth out of the said Parish they shall Pay one Shilling a Load which said Sums of five Shillings a Load and one Shilling a Load shall be Paid to the foreman of the Homage for Every Load Contrary to this Order for the benefit of the said Homage

Also we find and Present that no Sheep Shall be put on the Stubbles within the said Manor before the Nineteenth day of September upon the Penalty of Twenty Pence per Score and so in Proportion for any Greater or Lesser Quantitys

Also we find and Present that none of the Inhabitants of the said Parish shall put upon the Comons belonging to the said Parish Any sheep called Hebbers before the fourth day of July and no more than Six Sheep to a family shall be put thereupon and to Continue there no longer than the Nineteenth day of September following upon the Penalty of five Shillings a Head for Every Sheep found there Contrary to this Order

Also we find and Present that no Inmate or Person who is not a Parishioner shall put or keep any Cattle of Any kind upon the Comons or Wastes belonging to this Parish upon a Penalty of five Shillings a Head for all Cattle that shall be found there Contrary to this Order

From the Bottom of the Pile

Also we find and Present that every Inhabitant of this Parish shall Burnmark with his or her own Marks the Horses mares and Colts or Otherways Pitched on the Right Hip and the Horned Cattle either to be burned Marked on the Right Horn or Pitched on the Right Hip on the Penalty of five Shillings per Head for all such Horses mares colts or Horned Cattle that shall be found on the Comon not marked after Sixteenth day of May next

Also we find and Present that if any Customary Tenant of the said Manor shall Surrender any of his Customary Messuages or Tenements into the Hands of the Lord of the said manor by the Hands and Acceptance of any two such Messuage holders for the use of any other Person or Persons Absolutely without any Proviso or Condition that then such Tenants Taking Such Surrender by the Custom of the said Manor to Present such Surrender at the next Court Baron Holden for the said Manor after the Taking thereof

Also we find and Present that if any Person shall purchase Any Ancient Heriotable Messuage or Cottage within the said Manor and shall be Admitted tenant thereto that upon such Admittance unto such Messuage or Cottage he ought by the Custom of the said Manor to pay the Lord of the said Manor a fine only And not a Heriot for the Same

Also we find and Present that if any Customary Tenant of the said Manor shall Surrender any of his Customary or Copyhold Messuages or Tenements into the Hands of the Lord of the said Manor by the hands And Acceptance of any two such Messuage holders for the use and Behoofe of any Person or Persons under a Proviso or Condition in the same Surrender mentioned or Expressed for a Payment of a Certain sum of Money at a Day Limmited and Appointed for Payment thereof then if the said Sum of Money be not Paid at the time Limmited for Payment thereof then such Tenants taking such Surrender at the next Court Baron Holden for the said Manor after such Nonpayment of such Sum of Money and not before altho' the Lords of the said Manor should hold divers Courts Between the time Limmited therein for payment of such sum of Money as Aforesaid ought by the Custom of the said Manor to Present the said Surrender

Also we find and Present That if any Customary Tenant of the said Manor shall Surrender any of his Customary or Copyhold Messuages Lands or Tenements into the Hands of the Lord of the said Manor by the Hands and Acceptance of Any two such Messuageholders for the use and behoofe of Any other Person or Persons under a Proviso or Condition in the Same Surrender mentioned or Expressed that it shall be Lawfill for such Tenant making such Surrender to recall and make void such Surrender at any time during the Space of three Years next after the making thereof that then such Tenants taking such Surrender may by the Custom of the said Manor keep such Surrender in their Hands and not Present the same during the said Term of three Years if such Tenant making such Surrender live so long and not Revoke such Surrender that then such Tenants taking such Surrender ought by the Custom of the said Manor to Present such Surrender at the next Court Baron Held for the said Manor after the death of such Tenant dying as aforesaid and not before

Also we find and Present that no greene turfe shall be cutt upon the Comon or Waste ground in the said Manor or Parish on the Penalty of Ten Pounds to be paid to the foreman of the Homage for the use of the Poor of the Said Parish

Tho Weekly T Jarvis William Jarvis John Heath James Tillyer

Finally, at a meeting of the Parish Vestry held at the King's Arms Inn at Longford on 22nd June 1791 it was agreed *that a Strong House for the reception of felons and other Disorderly Persons*

Manorial Rules of Life

shall be built ---- on that part of the Waste between the gates of John Atlee's yard. The outside of the building was 10 feet (3m) square and the inside was 6ft 4in (1.93m) from floor to ceiling. The construction details were specified and it should have been adequately secure if prisoners had no tools to hand. Also there was a pair of stocks adjoining the house, *the roof of which shall extend over the Said Stocks and a bench for the Convenience of prisoners both within and without of the Said House and the same made secure with iron.*

In medieval times the Lord of the Manor played an active role in his domain. For example the term 'heriot' mentioned above refers to actions such as giving the Lord of the Manor your best ox in exchange for being allowed to occupy the same land worked by your recently deceased father. As England came out of the medieval period, and money became the main means of exchange, it seems that the Lord of the Manor gave up day-to-day control of his lands and tenants to his more prosperous families. This was in exchange for an income every time land or housing etc. changed hands. Thus we see above, the way in which men from the more prosperous families made up the Homage, made up laws for operation within the manor, created prisons and a workhouse, and controlled the Poor Law fund.

However the summary above is not intended to imply that the Lord of the Manor (in this case his wife) had no care for those living in their manor. On her return to England after her husband's tour of duty as Ambassador to the Turkish Empire, the Countess of Uxbridge established a medical practice for reducing the incidence of smallpox. More on this in the essay concerning William. Also after losing her husband the now dowager countess established a fund in 1748 for the relief of those who were poor, but did not receive Poor Law monies during the previous year.

Then, despite the harshness of much of life towards the end of the 18th century there is evidence of humanity by those in control in unexpected ways. An example of this concerns Mary, wife of William, when she was nearing term for the birth of one of her children. More on this in the essay concerning William. And finally one must recall that members of the Homage did all their community work on a volunteer basis. They received no direct financial reward for their civic activities. This does not mean that they were a purely altruistic group of men. When a member of the Homage took possession of land on behalf of the Lord of the Manor until the next Court Baron he could, and did, regard any harvest as his. And finally, how did the families comprising the Homage in the Manor remain as its most prosperous occupiers for a period of at least 250 years if their position did not confer on them a range of unassailable privileges?

In the year 1600 the population of England was about 3 millions, and periods of starvation were not uncommon. Also at that time one third of farm land under the plough was left fallow, and many animals were slaughtered in the autumn because they could not be fed during the winter months. As time progressed into the 18th century two developments occurred. Firstly the population increased and reached about 20 millions by the year 1800, and secondly the value of fertiliser was realised. The use of fertiliser enabled cattle etc. to be kept during the winter months, with their production of added fertiliser, but there was a view that to produce sufficient food for a growing population a change in the structure of land ownership and operation was needed. This led to a series of Enclosure Acts in which the present system of land tenure was brought into being. Harmondsworth was enclosed in 1819 and the consequences of the Enclosure Act brought much misery to the poorer people in the Manor. More on this in the essay concerning James.

Earliest recorded Forebears to mid-18th century

The ancestral fog begins to lift with a man born in about the year 1600. His name was Toucher Guydon and he was an ancestor of a Mary Guidon who was born in 1703. It is this Mary who married a Thomas Douton in 1725, and Thomas is the earliest ancestral Dowden that has been positively identified. During their married life Thomas and Mary lived in the hamlet of Heathrow which was part of the manor and parish of Harmondsworth.

It was in 1538 that churches were first required to keep records of all baptisms, births and burials. Many parishes do indeed have records back to that time, but sadly the Harmondsworth church records before 1670 have been lost. However on a yearly basis the incumbent in a church was required to send a summary of his activities to his bishop, and these records are known as the bishop's transcripts. Fortunately just a few of the bishop's transcripts for Harmondsworth in the 1630's survive, and these indicate that a Toucher Guydon had a son named Christopher baptised in St. Mary's Church in 1630.

Now 'Toucher' is not a normal English christian name and this led to a search of the Elizabethan records concerning 'strangers' or foreigners. This search indicates that in the 1590's a stranger with the name Supplie Guydon was living in London, and this implies that Supplie was a religious refugee. Also Supplie is recorded as paying taxes, so in the 1590's he was an established resident. From this it is inferred that he was a generation earlier than Toucher. Clearly the terms Supplie and Toucher translate from French to present-day English as 'beg' and 'to touch' and these can be regarded as religious terms in the form of 'supplicant' and 'one who touches'. This, in its turn, means that neither Supplie nor Toucher were Huguenot refugees because, according to the Huguenot Society, practices such as acting as a supplicant or touching in a religious manner were not part of Huguenot practice. This leaves the possibility, not proven, that Supplie was a member of a Wallonian church in London. It is also possible, that Supplie could have been be Toucher's father.

As an aside it is worth noting that the term 'guydon' was used in medieval times by the French to describe the man who stood next to his knight in battle and who held aloft the knight's pennant for use as a rallying point. In English the term 'guidon' is still used today, in this case for the (normally) triangular pennant at the top of a sailing vessel's main mast. The French also still use the term 'guidon'. It is the French for a bicycle's handlebars!

It is possible that a member of the Guydon family could have been resident in Harmondsworth in late Elizabethan times, and a misfortune affecting the Paget family provides a source of records regarding this possibility. During the later years of the reign of Queen Elizabeth, the Paget family were suspected of serious wrong-doing. As was the custom, suspicion of wrong-doing at this level in society resulted in the Paget family manorial holdings being confiscated by the Crown, and then returned later only if the suspicions were unfounded. In practice the holdings were later returned. However a consequence of the above was that in the year 1598,

From the Bottom of the Pile

Thomas, son of William Paget, caused an inventory to be made of all copy-hold tenants in the Manor of Harmondsworth during the preceding 40 years. The name Guydon does not appear in this record.

There is also no indication of a Douton, Dowden or similar in the above Harmondsworth record, and it is therefore proved that no-one from either of these branches of my family tree were resident at Harmondsworth before 1598.

As noted above, the baptismal name given in St. Mary's Church, Harmondsworth during 1630 to the son of Toucher Guydon was Christopher, and St. Christopher is the patron saint of travellers. Is this coincidence, or was the child's name chosen with reason? At this distance in time we cannot tell. In 1681 a widow named Faith Guidon was buried at St. Mary's Church, Harmondsworth. Also at that time there were other members of the Guidon family living in Harmondsworth. Bearing in mind the Poor Law impact on travel, it seems probable that Christopher and any other possible siblings lived out their lives in Harmondsworth, this being their 'settlement' parish. But can we deduce anything else about Toucher? Out of the political turmoil of the 1630's, the English Civil War between King Charles I and Parliament began in earnest in the 1640's. One side effect of the war was that in 1641 each male resident over 18 years of age in Harmondsworth was required to sign an 'Attestation' document in support of the parliamentary principle, and no Guydon, or reasonable variant on the spelling, is noted in this document (located in the House of Lords library). The inference is that either Toucher had died by 1641, or that he was a stranger, or that he, without certain others in his family, had moved on.

It is during the reign of Charles II that the next Guidon record can be found. In the 1660's and 1670's there was a 'Hearth Tax' on the number of fireplaces in a property. The very poor did not pay this tax, however records indicate that in the 1670's payment was made by a Richard Gydon for two fireplaces. At that time Richard was living in Longford, part of the Manor of Harmondsworth, and it is clear that Richard was a relatively prosperous man.

Returning now to the Harmondsworth parish church records, all those made from 1670 appear to be complete. However it is highly probable that not all church-based activities were recorded. In 1678 an Act of Parliament required the dead to be buried in woollen shrouds and further required a legal affidavit to be given regarding compliance with the law. The affluent were content to continue their use of linen shrouds and to pay a fine into the Poor Law fund. However woollen shrouds and affidavit costs were often beyond the means of the poor and hence many people disposed of their dead illegally and secretly. Of course the local men of authority would have known of, and hence must have condoned the practice. Some references indicate that this was because those condoning secret burials felt that they owed more to the living than to the dead. Others are of the view that as the very poor were buried at the expense of the parish, and hence with the use of the Poor Law fund, it paid the local men of authority to 'turn a blind eye'. This Act was not repealed until early in the 19th century. Additionally in the period 1694-1702 there was a tax on entries in the parish register. Nationally there was a

Earliest Recorded Forebears to mid-18th Century

sudden reduction in the number of baptisms and marriages registered in this period, and there is no reason to suspect that Harmondsworth was different in this regard to other locations.

Against the above background several generations of people named Guidon are included in the records of St. Mary's Church, Harmondsworth, in the period 1677 to 1731. In practice it is certain that not all people named Guidon and resident in the parish were noted in the church records. This is proved by certain surviving Court Baron copy-rolls, however these are 18th century 'omissions' in the church records and they do not impact on the Dowden family tree. Noted below is a summary of all people named Guidon (and variants) who are recorded as having spent at least a part of their lives in the Manor of Harmondsworth.

--1630	Christopher, son of Toucher Guydon baptised.
1670's	Richard Gydon paying Hearth Tax for two fireplaces.
26-12-1677	John, son of John and Elizabeth Guidon baptised.
19-11-1681	Faith Guidon, widow, buried.
05-06-1700	John Guidon, day labourer, married Elizabeth Bishop.
17-06-1700	Elizabeth, wife of John Guidon, mat-maker, buried.
02-04-1701	Elizabeth, daughter of John Guidon, labourer, and Elizabeth, baptised.
17-09-1703	Mary, daughter of John Guidon, labourer, and Elizabeth, baptised.
22-06-1708	John Guidon, mat-maker and poor, buried.
20-05-1725	John Guydon, labourer, buried.
19-01-1731	Elizabeth Guidon, widow, buried.

Additionally, though not included in the church record, Sarah Guidon, daughter of labourer John and Elizabeth was born after 1703. Sarah's name is given in the Court Baron record for 25th April 1726. Also a John Guidon is mentioned as the occupant of a property in a Court Baron paper dated 24th April 1738. A copy of this paper is noted as an ancestral document. After the year 1738 there is no further mention of a Guidon in the Manor of Harmondsworth.

1703 Mary became my direct ancestor after her marriage to John Douton in 1725. Working back, it is established that Mary was the daughter of John and Elizabeth (nee Bishop). Similarly it is established that Mary's father was baptised in 1677 and hence her grandparents were the John and Elizabeth who were buried in 1708 and 1700 respectively. But who was Mary's great grandfather? Given the dates above it is possible that Christopher could have been Mary's great grandfather, but then Christopher may have had a brother or brothers who are not in the record. However any possible brothers of Christopher would have been the children of Toucher, and hence Toucher is, beyond reasonable doubt, the 2* great grandfather of Mary. Thus Toucher Guydon, is my 8*great grandfather, and he is the earliest of my identified ancestors.

At this point in the family history record we first meet an actual event. And strangely, according to the history books, it could not have occurred. Going back into early history it was King

From the Bottom of the Pile

Edward the Confessor who established a custom that lasted for some 750 years, namely 'touching' his subjects for the King's Evil. The 'evil' in question was scrofula -- a skin disease with glandular swellings (a form of tuberculosis) that is associated with malnutrition. The idea was that because the King had been anointed, and was hence God's representative in his realm, he could 'touch' a subject with this disease and, by invoking God, the disease would be cured. From the record, the practice of 'touching' by the monarch was a regular activity until the reign of King William III and Queen Mary. History books then teach us that King William refused to continue the practice of 'touching' on the grounds that it was nothing more than a Catholic superstition. However it is also in the record (and I have seen the original certificate with my own eyes) that on 23rd June 1697 mat-maker John and his wife Elizabeth took part in a formal ceremony that included their being 'touched' by King William III for the Kings Evil. So much for the history books. (Perhaps the last sentence is a little unfair. Harmondsworth is close to Hampton Court and it seems possible that King William III gave way to local pressure, but did not 'touch' people, in other parts of his realm.) After the death of King William III the 'touching' practice was performed by Queen Anne, and then discontinued after her death.

Returning to mat-maker John we see above that he was noted as poor at the time of his death in 1708, and this means that he was given a paupers funeral at the expense of the Poor Law fund. I suspect that this means he was a man who commanded respect in his community, because it was normal at this time to bury the poorer dead 'secretly' in order to avoid the cost of a woollen shroud and an associated affidavit. It is possible to form a logical view on why John was poor. During John's lifetime all villages were largely self-sufficient, and we see from the Hearth Tax records that there were only 107 houses in the Manor of Harmondsworth whose occupants paid this tax. In modern language he had a very limited market for his product. But also at the time of mat-maker John's death the provisions of the Poor Law 43 Eliz. c2 would have applied. These provisions stated that "the father and grandfather, and mother and grandmother, and the children of every poor, old, blind, lame and impotent person, or any other poor person not being able to work, being of sufficient ability shall at their own charges relieve and maintain every such person as the justices shall direct". Subject to appeal, this provision in the Poor Law was rigidly enforced, and hence the Overseer of the Poor would have paid for John's funeral only if he was unable to demand its cost from John's above-noted relatives or, exceptionally, it was determined as 'the decent thing to do'.

With the death of mat-maker John in 1708 the story moves to his only recorded child, a son also named John who was born in 1677. It is with 1677 John that we first see recorded evidence of land occupancy. 1677 John lived until 1725, and at the time of his death he was the copyhold tenant of 2.5 acres of land. There is just one record known to exist concerning John's acquisition of land, and this is contained in the proceedings of a Court Baron of the Manor of Harmondsworth held on 22nd April 1723. The court was presided over by Peter Walter, Esquire, Steward to the Rt. Hon. The Earl of Uxbridge, and the original was written in Latin. To give a flavour of its place in my forebears history, a translation of part of its proceedings is noted overleaf.

Earliest Recorded Forebears to mid-18th Century

At this court it was found by the Homage that William Garstner, one of the customary tenants of this manor, outside this court, namely the twenty-first day of April in the year of our Lord 1722, surrendered into the lord's hands and acceptance of William Syms and John White, two other customary tenants of the same manor All that one customary acre of land lying and being in a certain Shot called Shepards Pool in the common field of the aforesaid manor called Harmondsworth Field, the land of Richard Combes being on the south side and the land of Robert Whittington being on the north side. To the use and behoof of the aforesaid John Guydon, his heirs and assigns forever. And now the aforesaid John came into this court and asked to be admitted to the premises. To whom the lord, by his aforesaid Steward, granted seisin thereof by the rod, to have and to hold the aforesaid premises with the appurtenances to the aforesaid John, his heirs and assigns, from the lord at the will of the lord according to the custom of the aforesaid manor by annual rent and services thence before owed and accustomed.

He gave the lord by way of fine two pounds and two shillings and so was admitted thereupon as tenant and did fealty.

Perhaps some of the above verbiage, albeit in English, should be explained. The term 'Lord' in line two refers to God, the term 'lord' refers to the Lord of the Manor. On 21st April 1722, William Garstner, a man in his twenties, wished (or was forced?) to divest himself of certain areas of copyhold land. One acre of that land, located as indicated above, was to be assigned to John Guidon. The decision to act in this matter was made on 22nd April 1722 and on that date William Syms and John White took possession of the land on behalf of the Lord of the Manor. However land transfer to new copyhold tenants could take place only at a meeting of a Court Baron, and as the previous meeting had been held on 16th April 1722, the next meeting was not scheduled until 22nd April 1723. Thus William Syms and John White had effective possession of the land given up by William Garstner for a year, and during this time they will have used this land for their own benefit. On transferring land from one tenant to another it was usual for both parties to be present at a Court Baron, and for the rod to be used by the Steward with both people involved in the land transfer, however on this occasion it seems that William Garstner was not present. The recorded procedure was that the Steward and John Guydon held opposite ends of the rod and the Steward said "My lord granteth to you and your heirs to hold at my lord's will after the custom of the manor." (i.e. to take possession of the land in question.) The Steward then bade John Guydon to put his hand on a bible and do fealty. John Guydon then said "I shall bear faith and truth to my lord of this manor and as for this land that I have taken to hold here of my lord in court and truly to pay the rents, suits and services that belongeth thereto as for the time that I shall occupy so God help me." John then kissed the book (i.e. bible) and thus became the tenant of the copyhold land in question. Incidentally, a 'Shot' was a cultivated strip in an open field, for 'behoof' read advantage and for 'seisin' read possession. And lastly, for 'fine' read fee.

The church record indicates that 1677 John Guidon and his wife Elizabeth had two daughters, 1701 Elizabeth and 1703 Mary. Court Baron documents show that John and Elizabeth also had a third daughter named Sarah. Additionally, at this time there was a John Guidon in the manor who would have been of a similar age to the three sisters. It seems probable therefore that

From the Bottom of the Pile

this youngest John Guidon was a son of John and Elizabeth. The point here is that the record indicates a significant event in the life of a John Guidon, but does not specify which John was affected. At a Court Baron held on 20th April 1724, Christopher Blunt, a local man of substance surrendered to the Lord of the Manor his cottage and appurtenances situated in Moor Lane Harmondsworth. The surrender of his copyhold property was made on that day in order to enable a Derick Stone and his wife to become the new copyhold tenants, and that was duly done in the manner described above. However, as specifically mentioned in the record, the reason for this transfer was to enable Derick Stone to gain admission to the property. But a John Guidon, until that date, was living in this property as a tenant of Christopher Blunt, and hence it seems probable that this John Guidon then lost his rented home. Was this 1677 John, or was it the young man who was probably John's son? The record does not answer this question, but in 1724 a younger John who was the son of 1677 John could not have been older than 20 years of age because the two daughters were 22/23 and 20/21 years of age respectively It therefore seems probable that it was 1677 John who lost his home at this time. As an aside, on several occasions I have walked along Moor Lane in Harmondsworth, and the above tale 'comes alive' on each occasion.

However, after the death of 1677 John, the younger John continued to live in Harmondsworth. There is a Court Baron paper from the year 1738 concerning the younger John Guidon, and this document is noted as an ancestral document.

1677 John Guidon is recorded as making his last Will (probably by dictation to a third party and validation with his mark) on 12th May 1725, and then dying later that day. He was 48 years of age and he left a widow, three unmarried daughters and probably a son. At the time of John's death, the church record states that he was a 'day labourer'. The Court Baron record, dated 25th April 1726, shows that John was the copyhold tenant of two separate acres of arable land and a half-acre of meadow. Also John is not indicated as a copyhold tenant of a cottage, and hence he rented his home from one of the manor's more substantial copyholders. From these details we can deduce certain aspects of John Guidon's life. By not being the copyhold tenant of a cottage it is possible that he did not have access to the four acres of land for domestic crops specified in the 1601 Poor Law Act. But we do not know the truth in this regard. What we do know is that John had copyhold tenancy of two separate one acre plots of arable land and a 0.5 acre of meadow land (see next essay for proof). This, in theory, gave John a voice in how the area of farmland in the manor was to be managed in the following year, but others also had a voice, and the majority view (in terms of land area) prevailed. The point is that John could not grow his preferred crops on his two acres of arable land. There was a 'farming community' decision as to which areas of land would (about one third) would lie fallow each year, which crops would be grown in the areas under cultivation, and on which dates the livestock, otherwise elsewhere, would be allowed to glean from the arable land from which the harvest had been taken. This last point meant that John, and others, could not grow a late-summer-sown crop in order to alleviate probable winter hardship. Also, in a period when there were no mechanical aids, and when soil fertility was maintained by leaving areas of land fallow as opposed to the use of

Earliest Recorded Forebears to mid-18th Century

manure and crop rotation, the area of land available to John was insufficient to meet the food and rent needs of his family. Hence, as noted in the church burial record, John was employed on a daily basis in other farmers fields. Employment on a daily basis when required by other farmers was both an uncertain and an oppressive way to make a living. When John could not work on his own land, other farmers would not require his services; similarly employment was most likely when John needed to work on his own land.

Before leaving 1677 John, perhaps his occupancy of land should be put into perspective. The Hearth Tax records of the 1670's and 1680's indicate that there were some 100 tax-paying households in Harmondsworth. Say, by way of pure speculation, that an equal number of households were poor enough to avoid the tax, and that every household had an area of land for purely domestic purposes of four acres, then some 800 acres of land in the manor were not available for agricultural activities. But the Manor of Harmondsworth occupied an area of about five square miles, i.e. some 3200 acres. Now 3200 - 800 = 2400, and if one divides 2400 by 100 (the number of Hearth Tax paying households) then each of these households would have been the copyhold tenants of some 24 acres. Of course at no time in known history has there been an equal distribution of land, however the arithmetic indicates that John's landholding of 2.5 acres was relatively trivial. In short, the larger copyhold tenants, determined what was to be done, and John, on his patch, had no effective say in the matter, and he had to comply.

In summary the record indicates that Toucher Guidon could not have been a long-term resident of Harmondsworth when his son Christopher was baptised in 1630. It would seem to follow that Toucher would not have been a substantial Harmondsworth copyhold landowner. In the late 17th century Toucher's grandson, mat-maker John, and also his wife Elizabeth, are 'touched' by King William III for the King's evil, this being a disease caused by malnutrition. Mat-maker John is later buried as a pauper. 1677 John fared a little better than his father, but appears to have lost his tenanted home when, for reasons unknown, it paid the copyholder landlord to transfer the copyhold ownership to a third party. Also, 1677 John's copyhold ownership of 2.5 acres of land did not give him freedom in relation to crop activity. In short, none of the Guidon's in the years up to the death of 1677 John in May 1725 had an easy life, even by the standards of their time.

As noted above, the second child of 1677 John and his wife Elizabeth was Mary, born in 1703. The history continues with what is known concerning Mary, her husband, and particularly one of their sons.

From the Bottom of the Pile

Thomas and Mary

The earliest Dowden's found in the record lived in London in late Elizabethan England. The reason for their being recorded is that they were fined for not attending church as required by law at that time. This shows an attitude of mind not untypical of later generations of Dowden's, but of course it does not provide proof of their being my forebears. Moving forward in time, in the 1670's a Jon Dowden paid Hearth Tax for one fireplace in his home at Harefield, a village some 10 miles (16km) north of Harmondsworth. Also in Harefield a John Dounton married an Elizabeth Grove on 16th July 1668. Given the non-standard spelling of names at that time it is probable that Jon and John were either the same person or would have been closely related, for example, father and son. On 16th September 1678 a Richard, son of Richard and Mary Dounton was baptised in Staines. We see therefore that in the late 17th century there were people with the surname Dowden, or variants, living within easy range of Harmondsworth. Moving to the early 18th century the following christenings are noted as occurring in relatively nearby East Molesey, Surrey.

Thomas Doudon	Marey Doudin	John Dowding	Benjamin and Joseph Dowdin
03-02-1701	17-07-1702	13-07-1704	12-03-1706

Edward Dowding	(male) Dowden	Benjamin Dowden.
23-06-1708	16-02-1712	13-02-1733.

The parents of Thomas are not noted, however the other christenings up to 1712 have John and Frances noted as parents, The parents of 1733 Benjamin were Joseph and Elizabeth, (presumably 1706 Joseph). It seems most probable that John and Frances were the parents of 1701 Thomas, and it is possible, but only possible, that he was the Thomas who married Mary Guidon in 1725.

Given now that the Poor Laws made it difficult for ordinary people to move far from their place of settlement it seems probable that the people noted above were related to my direct forebears, and hence also that they have a place on my family tree. It is at this point that the tracing of direct Dowden ancestors becomes very difficult. If a person moves from parish 'A' to parish 'B', and then forms part of the record for parish 'B', how can one prove that the individual in question came originally from parish 'A'? There is perhaps one possible answer, namely if an unusual Christian name is passed through the generations. In the Dowden case, the name Ralph is possibly a candidate, but no 17th century Ralph has been found in the record.

The reader may recall that in late Elizabethan times the Paget family were the Lords of the Manor of West Drayton as well as Harmondsworth. This was still the case in 1714 when the then head of the Paget family was created The Earl of Uxbridge. Following his elevation to the peerage the earl was appointed as the King's Ambassador to the Sultan of Turkey, and hence he and his wife spent several years in Constantinople. Following their return home the Countess encouraged in the Earl's manors a medical practice previously unknown (or at least unused)

From the Bottom of the Pile

in England at that time, but common practice in Turkey. This practice had an impact on at least one of my forebears two or three generations later, but more on this matter in the essay including this individual. Suffice it note here that from 1714 on, the Lord of the Manor of Harmondsworth, and also West Drayton, was the Rt. Hon. The Earl of Uxbridge.

It was on 12th May 1725 that John Guidon died, leaving his 2.5 acres of land between his three daughters Elizabeth, Mary and Sarah. Then on 9th August 1725, his second daughter Mary Guidon married a Thomas Downtown in the Church of St. Mary the Virgin in West Drayton, and at the time of his marriage Thomas was employed by the Earl of Uxbridge as a 'porter and dr(?)'. (The term 'dr' probably refers to drayman, in which case Thomas was employed moving items by hand or horse-driven cart from one location to another.) Then also, because Mary's father John died after the Court Baron meeting in April 1725 the transfer of inherited land to Mary could not be completed until 1726. Noted below is a translation from Latin of the proceedings of the Court Baron held in Harmondsworth in 1726.

Manor of Harmondsworth in the county of Middlesex

Court Baron of the Right Honourable Henry, Earl of Uxbridge, lord of the aforesaid manor held on the 25th day of April in the twelfth year of the reign of George I, by the grace of God, King of Great Britain, France and Ireland and in the year of our Lord 1726, by Peter Walter Esquire, Steward there.

James Tillear Henry Youle William Wild Christopher Blunt

Richard Combes John White John Atlee

Sworn

At this court it was found by the Homage that John Guidon one of the customary tenants of this manor outside the court namely, on the twelfth day of May last past, surrendered into the lord's hands through the acceptance of James Tillear and William Syms and two other customary tenants of the same manor All his customary lands within the aforesaid manor to the use set out in his last Will. And that the aforesaid John made his last Will in writing bearing the date twelfth day of May aforesaid and by the same bequeathed in words to the effect following namely, 'I give and bequeath to my daughter Mary my one acre of copyhold land lying in Shepistone Field in a shot called Little Acres after the first crop is taken of after the date hereof' as by the same Will he makes clear and apparent. And now the aforesaid Mary, now the wife of Thomas Downton came into this court and asked to be admitted to the premises. To whom the lord, by his aforesaid Steward, has granted seisen thereof by the rod, to have and to hold the aforesaid premises with the appurtenances to the aforesaid Mary according to the aforesaid Will from the lord at the will of the lord according to the custom of the aforesaid manor by annual rent and services thence before owed and accustomed. She gave the lord by way of fine one pound fifteen shillings. And so was admitted thereupon as tenant etc.

In practice both 1701 Elizabeth and 1703 Mary were married during the period between the death of their father John Guidon and the Court Baron meeting some eleven months later. Elizabeth married a Joseph Tomkins (also spelt Tombyns), a man who was legally settled in the parish of Harmondsworth. Elizabeth also retained, in her name only, the copyhold tenancy of the one acre of land bequeathed by her father. Sarah was given possession of the 0.5 acre of meadow-land but, because she was still a minor in 1726, the land was placed under the control of her mother during Sarah's minority. Mary was also bequeathed one acre of land by her father, and she could have retained ownership of her land as was legal at the time. But she and her new husband had other matters to consider. Her husband Thomas was born outside the parish of Harmondsworth and hence his place of settlement was elsewhere. Despite Mary marrying Thomas in the parish of his place of work (but possibly not settlement), namely West Drayton, it is clear that they wished to live their married lives in the parish of Harmondsworth. How could this be achieved? The answer was for Mary to give to Thomas 5/6 of her newly acquired acre of land By this means Thomas could meet the conditions of Poor Law legislation in order to be regarded as now being 'settled' in the parish of Harmondsworth. This may read as being simple, but the law of the time required the Steward to 'examine' anyone, who appeared to be giving up land for no financial return, in order to satisfy himself that this was not being done under duress. And importantly, Mary was pregnant at the time of the Court Baron in 1726. At the 1726 Court Baron, Mary stated that she wished to give to her husband the 5/6 acre mentioned above, and the record indicates that she was 'examined' by the Steward, in a separate and private room, in order to determine that her wishes were not being made under duress. At this point we meet a concept not familiar to us today. John Guidon was the copyhold tenant of 2.5 acres, and all this land was ultimately owned by the lord of the manor. Thus Mary could only give to Thomas 1/3 of the 2.5 acres owned by the lord of the manor. It follows that $1/3 * 2.5 = 5/6$, but the point of ultimately who owns what is made. A translation from Latin of the Court Baron procedures in which Mary gave 5/6 of her acre of land to Thomas is given below.

At the aforesaid court sitting, the aforesaid Thomas Downton together with Mary his wife, in full and open court according to custom (the same Mary being first examined alone and secretly by the Steward and thereupon consenting) surrendered into the lord's hands by the hands and acceptance of the aforesaid Steward All that aforesaid acre and third part of two and a half acres of which the aforesaid John Guidon died seized To the use and behoof of Mary for the term of her natural life and after the death of the aforesaid Mary, then to the use of the aforesaid Thomas his heirs and assigns forever. And now the aforesaid Mary asked to be admitted to the premises. To whom the lord, by his aforesaid Steward granted seisin thereof by the rod, to have and to hold the aforesaid premises with appurtenances to the aforesaid Mary and Thomas in the manner and form aforesaid from the lord at the will of the lord according to the custom of the aforesaid manor by annual rent and services thence before owed and accustomed. And the aforesaid Mary was admitted thereupon as tenant etc.

In the section named Ancestral Documents is noted a copy of an original paper found during a search through surviving documents of the Earl of Uxbridge from the early 18th century. The paper is a financial summary of the transactions of the Court Baron held on the 25th April 1726. Until the chance discovery of this paper, at the London Metropolitan Archive, I (Brian Dowden) had no idea as to the maiden name and hence forebears of Mary. The thrill of finding this document, and of holding in my hand a paper written some 280 years previously that concerned my forebears, gave my wife Sheila and I a thrill that is beyond description.

From the Bottom of the Pile

The supposition above, to the effect that Mary's sharing with her husband Thomas 5/6 of her one acre of land gave him settlement rights, appears to be substantiated some 11 years later. In a record dated 8th March 1737/8 it is noted that Thomas Dowton was assessed to pay 1s 8d (8.3p) for the poor as a result of his tenancy in Shepistone (now called Sipson). The land on which this charge was based was almost certainly the plot inherited by Mary in 1726.

As noted above, Mary 'Downton' was some six months pregnant when she gained possession of her father's one acre of land in April 1726. Her first child, a daughter also named Mary, was baptised at St. Mary's Church Harmondsworth on 7th August 1726. At baby Mary's baptism the surname is recorded as Doutton, while at the baptisms of Mary's later siblings the spellings Dowton and Douton are used. Also, to add to the spelling conundrum, a Charles and Elizabeth Dowten were present at the baptism ceremony held for Christopher Douton in 1740. There appear to be two possible reasons for the inconsistency in the spelling of the surname of Thomas and Mary. The first reason is that before the average person could read and/or write, clerks who did not personally know the people involved in ceremonies such as baptisms simply wrote what they felt they heard. In Harmondsworth this lack of personal knowledge occurred after 1727. Between 1713 and 1727 a Thomas Tyson was the last vicar living at Harmondsworth. His successor, John Lidgould, lived at West Drayton, and it appears that for the remainder of the 18th century the church at Harmondsworth was served by a succession of curates who provided a very limited range of services. It seems probable therefore that different curates, not familiar with Thomas and Mary, spelt their surname as they felt fit, and this was not challenged by the illiterate Thomas and Mary. In 1729 when Elizabeth, the second child of Thomas and Mary was baptised it was noted that Thomas was an agricultural labourer. This means that he had left the employ of the Earl of Uxbridge. He continued to be described thus as each of his later children were baptised. Also, from 1729, the place of abode of Thomas and Mary is noted as being at Heathrow. Clearly Thomas and Mary were successful in their endeavours to establish the parish and Manor of Harmondsworth as Thomas' place of settlement.

With the establishment of Thomas and Mary at Heathrow it is perhaps interesting to note the origin of their home's place name. The name goes back to medieval times and it refers to the hamlet or row of cottages built at the edge of a heath or common land, in this case the western edge of Hounslow Heath. Substantial farmers would want their labourers to live as close as possible to, but not to occupy, productive farmland, and hence the location, and hence the name.

Thomas lived until 1747 and during their 22 years of married life Mary gave birth to eight children. Their family details are:

Thomas Downton, date of birth not certain (but possibly 1701 in East Molesey), died in 1747.
Mary Guidon/Downton, was born on 17-09-1703, but her date of death is unknown.
Their children were born/baptised on the dates noted overleaf:

Thomas and Mary

Mary	Elizabeth	Thomas	John
7-8-1726	22-6-1729	7-9-1730	18-2-1732
	10-8-1729		

Ralph	Elisabeth	Christopher	Sarah
30-5-1734	28-12-1737	18-3-1740	12-5-1745
			12-7-1747

Thomas and Mary Dowton are the earliest 'Dowden' forebears whose complete family structure is known. They are also the first to live in the hamlet of Heathrow. In practice one of their following four generations also lived in Heathrow, until at least the early years of the 20th century. No details of the day-to-day existence of Thomas and Mary have survived, but there are some records regarding the fate of their children. 1730 Thomas successfully established himself in a location some 8 miles (13 km) east of Harmondsworth. 1732 John lived his life in the Manor of Harmondsworth and he, with his wife, produced 10 children. 1734 Ralph lived in Heathrow for the majority of his life, and he is the subject of the next essay. 1729 Elizabeth and 1745 Sarah died while very young, while 1737 Elisabeth and 1740 Christopher disappear from the record.

Thomas and Mary followed an established tradition with regard to the naming of at least most of their children. Firstly they were given only one Christian name, and then the given name was also that of family member from a previous generation. People from the previous generation with six of the above names can be identified but what is the situation concerning the other two, namely Ralph and Christopher? What is clear from searching 17th and 18th century baptismal records is that the names Ralph and Christopher were very unusual. The name Christopher could have come from the Guidon side of the family because it is possible that Mary's grandfather remembered 1630 Christopher, but what about Ralph? In the absence of a Ralph in the Guidon record it seems probable that the name Ralph, if it came from a forebear, would have come from the Douton side of the family, and hence, if a 17th century Ralph Douton can be found within an area of, say, 20 miles radius of Harmondsworth, then Thomas Douton's forebears will have been traced. But no Ralph Douton (or similar surname) has been found.

From educational and legal viewpoints Thomas and Mary would have been severely disadvantaged. The Quakers school in Harmondsworth, established in 1694, had failed, and no replacement is recorded until the late 18th century. Thomas and Mary were hence, almost certainly, illiterate. The legal system was designed so that normal people had to be to be self-supporting and hence humble folk, not being rich, had no meaningful opportunity for redress in law. The area of land of only one acre held by Thomas and Mary meant that their survival depended upon Thomas working for others as an agricultural labourer. However each villager had a domestic plot as described previously, and in addition there were 'common land' rights. These rights, dating back to Saxon times, and regarded as inviolable, included the right to graze livestock on the common land and to gather material such as brushwood for fuel. In

From the Bottom of the Pile

Harmondsworth, the Lord of the Manor was unusually generous in that he allowed his 'settled' residents to fish in all the rivers and common waters within the manor on Wednesdays, Fridays and Saturdays. And this fishing was for food, not sport.

As noted above, Thomas Dowton died and was buried in Harmondsworth in 1747. There is no record of the ultimate fate of Mary. A not uncommon practice in the 18th century was for the first partner in a marriage who died to be given a 'decent' burial because the surviving partner felt that this was something that he/she had to do. However when the second partner died the younger generation did not feel it necessary, or could not afford to pay the price of a woollen shroud and affidavit as required by the 1679 Burial Act. This resulted in the 'secret burials' as mentioned previously. From this it is inferred that Mary survived her husband and that her body was buried 'secretly' in the cemetery at St. Mary's Church Harmondsworth after her death.

It is Thomas and Mary's 5th child/3rd son named Ralph, born in 1734, who became the direct ancestor of the writer of this series of essays.

Ralph and Families

Before 1750 the family name is recorded by successive scribes as Downtown, Downton, Doutton, Douton and Dowton. After this date the name occurs mainly as Dowden. This difference may simply be the reflection of a change in regional accent or the letter of the alphabet used to represent a particular sound. Be that as it may, it seems somehow homely to use (mainly) the spelling I use today for my surname.

In the last essay the eight children of Thomas and Mary Douton are noted. Three of these children, namely 1731 John, 1734 Ralph and 1737 Elisabeth lived out their lives in the Manor of Harmondsworth. It is Ralph who was the writer's 3*greatgrandfather.

On 25th December 1760, an Elizabeth Dowden married a Joseph Mocock in St. Mary's Church, Harmondsworth. The bride in question was the 1737 Elisabeth noted above, and, as if to emphasise the random nature of spelling the bridegroom signed his name as Moocock. The record then indicates that Joseph and Elizabeth had several children during the following years. Note please that Joseph Moocock signed his name at his wedding, i.e. he was literate. This alone probably means that his social situation was above that of the illiterate agricultural labourer. In practice neither Joseph nor Elizabeth appear in the Poor Law records of the time, and this means that their financial circumstances were better than those of Elizabeth's brothers, John and Ralph.

On 13th October 1759 Ralph Dowden's elder brother John married a Mary Roberts in the church at Harmondsworth. It seems possible that the above Joseph and John's sister Elizabeth were courting at that time because one of the witnesses at John' wedding was Joseph Morecock! John and his wife Mary lived out their lives together at Longford, a settlement within one to two miles (1.5-3km) from both Heathrow and the centre of the village of Harmondsworth. They had ten children, namely: 30-11-1760 William, 18-4-1762 Joseph (died 4-12-1825), 5-10-1764 Jenny, 19-10-1766 John, 15-10-1769 Sarah, ?-1-1772 Rachel, 24-4-1774 Mary, 1-10-1775 Gorge (spelling as recorded and died 14-11-1782), 27-9-1778 Ann, and 2-12-1781 James (died 4-9-1818). Church records indicate the burial of John Dowden on 15th February 1789. His widow Mary survived until October 1817. There is no (known) record of John as a landowner, however he is noted as both a payer of tax and as a recipient of money from the Poor Law fund.

John's younger brother Ralph also moved to Longford for a short period of time, after which he returned to Heathrow until his death in 1810. But returning now to the mid-18th century the marital-cum-family status of Ralph left much to be desired as far as the vicar of St. Mary's Church Harmondsworth was concerned. Perhaps the starting point should be the church record. This states that on 6-2-1755 a child named Jhon was born to Ralph Dowden and Mary Sears, implying that Ralph and Mary were not married at the time of the birth. This child appears to have died shortly after his birth. Then on 16-5-1756 a child named Thomas, also born to Ralph Dowden and Mary Sears, was baptised in St. Mary's Church. To the church at the time, the production of an illegitimate child was a serious sin. For Ralph and Mary to transgress with Jhon was bad enough, but then to repeat the carnal exercise with Thomas was beyond beyond etc. Then, with no indication that Mary Sears was settled in Harmondsworth, why did the civil authorities not forcibly take Mary back to her place of settlement before the birth of these children? Perhaps, in a manner recognised by the civil authority, but not by the church, Ralph and Mary were in practice married.

Now the church in Harmondsworth may have regarded the two children of Ralph and Mary to be illegitimate or, in the language of the day, bastards. But importantly, Ralph was noted as the father of these children and hence was supporting his family. Also, for Mary, a 1744 amendment to the Poor Law would have come to her rescue. This Amendment ended the barbarity of carting (literally by forcible tying to carts) heavily pregnant women from parish to parish in order to avoid a bastard child becoming a burden on the expelling parish's Poor Law fund. The 1744 Act stated:- 'In the case of bastardy, and if the mother is considered a vagrant, a bastard child will be allocated to its mother's place of residence'. Previously the child was regarded as being 'settled' in the birth parish and hence the forcible removal of a heavily pregnant mother-to-be from parish to parish. Additionally, and specifically mentioned, The Amendment did not excuse the father from his obligation to support his child. If the civil authorities mirrored the church attitude, then either Ralph must have to be seen to support his family or, very quickly, Mary would have been considered a vagrant by Ralph's parish. And as a vagrant, Mary, with her children, would have been forced back to her place of settlement (Hayes) and been subject to the rigours of the Poor Law. Fortunately for Mary, it seems clear that Ralph was able to support both her and their children.

It is perhaps worth noting that at this time Poor Law aid to married people was proving to be more costly than aid to single people. This was because a single person usually had no children. Thus in order to minimise Poor Law expenditure, many parishes decided to discourage marriage by the very poor by demolishing part of the housing stock normally occupied by such people. There is no record of such an activity in Harmondsworth, but clearly Ralph and Mary were swimming in a very cruel sea.

Later records indicate that 1756 Thomas, son of Ralph, and 1760 William, son of John, moved to Hayes and spent the remainder of their lives in that location. The records then indicate descendants of both Thomas and William living in Hayes until at least the latter part of the 19th century. The search above led to an examination of the records of the parish church in Hayes, and this yielded the following: 'On 1st April 1734, Mary, the daughter of John and Ann Sears of Hayes Middlesex was baptised. The date matches perfectly with Ralph who was also baptised in 1734. It seems beyond reasonable doubt that Ralph's Mary Sears was the lady from Hayes.

Until to the mid-18th century the act of becoming married simply depended on a verbal contract. A marriage in a church, with the need for banns, a wedding ceremony and a subsequent church record was preferred by society, but not all citizens accepted or could afford this procedure. Alternatively one could marry within the precincts of certain prisons, because from at least medieval times such marriages were legal. These marriages avoided the need for banns and the costs associated with church-based ceremonies, but they were clandestine from the viewpoint of local authorities and the established church. Also, for reasons of personal secrecy, many people gave false names when marrying via this procedure, and this was far more difficult in a church-based marriage. North of the River Thames in London the grounds (outside the walls) of the Fleet Prison were used for such marriages, and they were conducted by men regarded as 'disreputable' clergy. However, records of their marriage activities were made. By the middle of the 18th century there were a significant number of people marrying in this way, and such marriages were regarded as weakening the social fabric of society and the bonds of marital morality. In short, the lower orders are getting away with something, and hence it must be stopped. The result was the Marriage Act 1753 which came into force on 26th March 1754. Under the Act a marriage had to be preceded by banns within the churches of both the bride and groom on three consecutive Sundays and the purchase of an official marriage licence (then costing £2-10s or £2-50p against a labourer wage of about 8s or 40p a week). Both participants had to be 21 years or older or have parental consent, the marriage had to be conducted by an authorised clergyman, it had to occur in front of witnesses, and finally it had to be be recorded in the church register. None of the above applied in a 'Fleet Prison' marriage.

Coming now to Ralph and Mary, on 8th July 1753 there is a Fleet record of a marriage of a James Stevens to a Mary Sears from Hayes. On 12th March 1754 there is a further Fleet record of the marriage of Ralph Dowden to a Sarah Sars. (i.e. Sears?) Notice here that the 'Ralph' marriage occurred only 13 days before the end of Fleet marriages and that in 1755 and 1756 the church is not recognising Ralph as being married to the mother of his sons Jhon and Thomas. A search has been made for a James Stevens, and none can be found. So is it then reasonable to accept that Mary Sears was indeed married to a real James Stevens in 1753? The answer must be 'yes' because the apparent absence of a record proves nothing. But is it also reasonable to accept that on two occasions Ralph allowed himself to be registered as the father of James and Mary's children if this was not the case? It seems unlikely. Indeed it seems possible that the name James Stevens was simply being used as a non de plume by Ralph Dowden. This thought is then reinforced by the fact that 1760 William, son of 1731 John, and 1755 Thomas, son of Ralph, both emigrated to Hayes and that they established themselves in that town. This seems most unlikely if Ralph was simply the 'fall guy' of a real James Stevens. In short, I think it probable that it was Ralph who married Mary Sears at The Fleet on 8th July 1753. Coming now to 12th March 1754, who was the Sarah Sars who married Ralph Dowden at The Fleet? To the writer it seems possible that Ralph and Mary were indeed a unit, and that Ralph had a pet name for his partner. Perhaps this pet name was 'Suh', and hence Sarah and Sars. But if the above represents the truth of the case, why undertake two 'Fleet' marriages? I suspect, but cannot prove, that the use by Ralph of the name James Stevens in 1753 got him into hot water with his local authorities, and hence a 'marriage' in 1754 in his own name. But this does not explain the attitude of the church in 1755 and 1756.

There is however a later occurrence that may invalidate much of the above. Ralph's son 1771 William married a Mary in 1795, and in 1798 their eldest daughter was named Sarah. At that time it was common practice to name children after their forebears which implies that 1798 Sarah may have been named after her paternal grandmother. If this was the case, then it makes a proper understanding of the above events even more difficult. In the family tree section of the Ralph Dowden record, Mary Sears and Sarah Sars are noted as two separate people - as per the church record.

Following the uncertainty inherent in the above events, Ralph and his wife 'Sarah' had four more children, namely 1-3-1759 Elizabeth, 11-4-1762 Mary, 11-11-1764 Jane and ?-8-1771 William. Each was noted in the parish record as being the child of Ralph and Sarah Dowden. It was 1771 William who was to become my 2* great grandfather.

On 2nd August 1788 Ralph stole nine hempen sacks, value 5s-0d (25p), the property of a Robert Singer. The record suggests that it was a clear-cut case because the sacks in question were found in Ralph's house. Ralph was sentenced to six months imprisonment, but the record does not say where. At that time Ralph was 54 years of age and his children were all of working age. Presumably they must have looked after their mother during Ralph's period of incarceration. From this incident we see something of interest about relative values. Those nine sacks were worth about £15-00 each in terms of today's money.

On 23-6-1790 Ralph's wife Sarah is recorded as being buried. They had been married for some 37 years. The church record coldly states: 'Sarah Douden was drounded'. There is no indication in the record as to why Sarah drowned. It is possible that domestic water was drawn from a well, but it is also possible that water for home use would have been taken from a local pond or river. Avoiding conspiracy theories, one can only presume that Sarah slipped into a pond or local river and could not swim.

In 1799, Ralph remarried, he was then 65 years of age. His new wife was 7 months pregnant at the time of their marriage and two months later (baptised 24-11-1799) a son named James was born. Perhaps the Christian name of Ralph's new wife is of interest, it was Kerrenhapuch. It was common practice during the 18th century that when a poor family brought a child to church for its baptism the minister would 'suggest' a name for the child. And the poor family found themselves having to accept the suggestion. If one looks at chapter 42 verse 15 in the King James version of Book of Job, Kerrenhapuch was one of three daughters described as 'the fairest in the land'. During the following years Ralph's wife presented him with two daughters. They were 19-9-1802 Roza and 5-10-1806 Phillis. Ralph finally died in 1810 at the age of 76 years leaving adult offspring from his first marriage, a widow, and three young children from his second marriage. Difficult times were ahead for his young family, but more of this in the next essay. The church record notes Ralph as being 81 years age at his death. It seems he was proud of his extraordinary old age and hence exaggerated the same. He lived in a tough age and I hope he died with a smile on his lips. Kerrenhapuch, as a widow, survived for another 28 years and was buried in 1838.

Ralph and Families

Returning now to earlier times, in 1748, Elizabeth, Dowager Countess of Uxbridge invested £100-00 in a fund for the poor in the Manor of Harmondsworth. The idea was that each year a sum of £3-00 would be shared between ten or twelve of the poor families in the manor who had not received parish relief. The money was distributed each January. To put this into year 2010 terms, the minimum wage is £5-80p an hour. And based on a 40 hours work this adds to £232-00 each week. In the mid-18th century the poor labourer worked far more hours in a week for a wage of not more than 8s-0d or 40p a week. And £232-00 and 40p differ by a factor of 580. So if ten families shared £3-00 from the Dowager Countess, it was worth about £174-00 for each family in our money. There were no payments to a member of the Dowden family in the years 1748 to 1758, then the following payments were made to either Ralph or to his elder brother John.

1759 Ralph Douden, Longford, 5s-6d (27.5p)

1762-68 Ralph Dowden, (no given location), 6 times 5s-6d, and 4s-6d in 1765.

1770, 72, 73, 75, 78, 79,84, 86, John Dou/wden 5s-6d or 5s-0d each year.

1794 Widow Dowden 5s-0d. (John Dowden, Ralph's brother died in 1789.)

The next set of records concern tax payments made by John Dowden and a sum paid into or received from the parish rates. These are (or perhaps now were) held by William Wild, a descendant of twelve generations of that name and born in Harmondsworth.

October 1766 to 5th April 1757, paid 1s-6d + 1s-6d tax. This sum, totalling 15p in today's money is noted in a 'windows and lights' account.

5th August 1767, paid or received 2s-2.25d (11p) into or from the Poor Law fund. There is room for confusion in this privately owned record, but if it was for relief then Thomas Weekly and John Mash (Overseer of the poor) held the purse strings.

5th April 1768 to 5th April 1770   paid 3s-0d Window Tax.

5th April 1770 to 5th April 1771   paid 3s-0d Window Tax.

5th April 1772 to 5th April 1773   paid 3s-0d Window Tax.

The Churchwarden's accounts cover payments made to paupers during the period 1785 to 1863 and note:

8th November 1787	J. Dowden,	5s-0d
7th March 1788	J. Dowden,	5s-0d
1788 to 1789	J. Dowden,	5s-0d, 5s-0d, 5s-0d, 5s-0d, 10s 6d, and 5s-0d.

It seems probable that the above payments were made as a consequence of John's state of health, bearing in mind that he died in 1789. John's widow Mary then received payments as noted below:

1789 Widow Dowden, Longford, 1s-0d, and then:

1792, 17-02-1797, 28-04- 1??? (between 1797 and 1800), 07-01-1801, 09-01-1805 and 05-12-1806, five payments of 5s-0d and then one of 7s-0d.

From the Bottom of the Pile

Ralph and family were also recipients of money as follows:

1788-89   Ralph Dowden's wife, 2s-6d.

16-04-1800 and 07-01-1801   Ralph Dowden, two payments of 5s-0d.

A privately owned record indicates that in 1797 Ralph was both the proprietor and the occupier of a parcel of land. The record states:

19th June 1797,	Ralf Dowden	Proprietor,	£1-0s-0d land tax.
	Ralph Dowden	Occupier	£4-0s-0d land tax.

The sums above paid by Ralph formed the basis for future assessments according to the Land Tax Act of 1798. At this time the UK was in the throes of war with revolutionary France, and hence the Act encouraged landowners to pay more tax today on the promise of a worthwhile rebate tomorrow. The scheme was that if a landowner paid 15 years assessment in a lump sum, then he would be exempt from all future land taxes to be levied under the Act. The inference of this is that Ralph would have to pay 15*£5-0s-0d = £75-0s-0d for the exemption and there is no known record of such a sum being paid. Another document (reported to, but not seen by me) shows Ralph paying 4s-0d land tax in 1798, and then, from the above, we see that Ralph's wife received 2s-6d in parish relief during 1788-89. Clearly Ralph's finances led an up and down existence.

Noted above are some of the payments made from the Churchwardens accounts. Other payments, not of a charitable nature also placed a burden on the churchwardens finances. During the late 18th-early 19th centuries period the churchwardens made many payments for what can only be described as the wholesale slaughter of a selection of the local wildlife. For example in 1786 they paid £1-12s-9d for 131 dozen (1572) sparrows, 2s-8d for six hedgehogs and two polecats. A year later they paid £2-9s-3d for 197 dozen sparrows, 2s-4d for 7 hedgehogs and 2s-8d for 8 polecats. A small part of this record names a James Dowden who was paid 1s-6d for 72 sparrows. James was the youngest child of John and Mary and was 13 years of age at the time. If James was living with his widowed mother, the money would have been a very useful addition to family income.

The final documents recording events late in the life of Ralph are the Vestry Minutes. These minutes are in private possession and, although I have seen them and indeed have some photocopies, I have no knowledge as to the owner of these papers. The Vestry Committee members were the leading citizens in the Manor of Harmondsworth, and it was this committee that received the manorial rates income and then paid for local works (e.g. road repair) and allocated money to the needy poor. The authority of the committee was not however limited to purely financial matters as can be seen below. To provide a flavour of the extent of this committee's activities the following notes are grouped as indicated.

Ralph and Families

Prices and wage levels.

25-04-1791 Cost of flower (flour) is £6-0s-0d per sack (quantity not specified) and meat is 6d per pound (approx. 6p per kilogram).

23-05-1792 Ordered that men working on the highway do work eight hours for 1 shilling.

17-05-1797 Ordered that men employed by the Surveyors to work from 6 o'clock to 3 o'clock to have 1s-6d per day.

Property and general Poor Law administration.

03-02-1790 Agreed that the partition between the two rooms next to the Dowden's house be took down and it is further agreed that there is a grate put up in the great room. (It is unlikely that there would have been a grate in the Dowden's house at that time.)

[A parish could gain ownership of a dwelling via the Poor Law. A copyhold tenant asking for parish relief could receive same on condition that on death his/her cottage passed into the ownership of the parish. This may have occurred in the property next door to the Dowden's.]

Frequently in the record:

Agreed that stock money approved for payment to (name given) to be made only if (name) has his dog destroyed. [The vestry committee was willing to support someone in sufficient need, but it was not prepared to see one penny spent on the welfare of the claimants dog. Also in the period 1796 to 1882 there was a tax levied on the possession of a dog, and clearly the vestry committee was not prepared to accept any responsibility for paying this tax.]

09-05-1792: Agreed to pay Joseph Dowden living with Mrs. Stent, and James Hill living with Mr. Atlee £1-11s-6d each on account of their being drawed for the Militia. [Joseph was a son of John and Mary, and was born in 1762. The militia in question was the County Militia, not unlike the Territorial Army today. Probably Joseph would have been displeased by his 'conscription' because at that time respectable working people regarded enlistment into the army a sign of failure in life, if not indeed a positive disgrace. The nature or locations of Joseph's service are not in the local records, but suffice it to say that he survived the Napoleonic Wars and died in 1825.]

John Dowden's widow - Mary.

31-10-1792 Ordered that Widdow Dowden be charged £1-0s-0d in the rates.

02-01 1795, 02-03-1796,
& 18-01-1797 Ordered that Widdow Dowden have 5s-0d stock money.

08-01-1800 The Widdow of John Dowden living at Nine (Elms?) to be allowed 3s-0d per week to Lady Day for the keep of her three children to be paid by Mr. Riddington. (Who was a member of the Vestry Committee.)

From the Bottom of the Pile

23-03-1807   Ordered Widw. Dowden 2s-0d ??? Week. (The ??? note refers to a shorthand comment that could be All- and hence Allowance.)

Ralph and Kerrenhapuch Dowden.

07-01-1801   Ralp Dowden 5s-0d stock money.
Dame Dowden 5s-0d stock money.

25-05-1801   Ralp Dowden surrendered himself to Mr. Riddington to be supported at the Workhouse. (Ralph was 67 years of age at this time.)

14-10-1801   Agreed that Ralf Dowden's wife have half a Crown (2s-6d) of the overseers.

02-06-1802   Lydia Taylor applied for assistance for Ralf Dowden's wife.

From the above it seems that the life of Ralph and Kerrenhapuch was far from easy, even by the standards of the day.

As noted above, Ralph died in 1810 at 76 years of age. After the above 1802 record, nothing further is known about the details of the life of Kerrenhapuch. Perhaps this is not surprising because of the unusual name she was given as a child, and the fact that she was later known as Cary or Katherine. As noted, Kerrenapuch died in 1838.

William and Mary

William, my 2* great grandfather, and son of Ralph, was born in 1771. He appears to have spent all his life living at Heathrow in the parish and manor of Harmondsworth.

In the essay concerning Ralph, the 'muddle' relating to Ralph's marriage or marriages outside the Fleet Prison were noted. A 'reasonable' interpretation of the record appears to indicate that Mary Sears and Sarah Sars were the same person. Additionally it is known that Mary Sears was the daughter of John and Ann Sears and was baptised in the parish church at Hayes on 1st April 1734. Following the births of Ralph's eldest surviving son 1756 Thomas, and brother John's eldest son 1760 William, we know that these cousins spent their adult lives living in Hayes. Indeed later records from Hayes show that on 21st April 1829 a Thomas Dowden and aged 73 years was buried, and that in the 1841 census mention is made of a William Dowden aged 81 years. These ages correspond exactly to 1756 Thomas and 1760 William. In short, a link between John and Ralph and their sons Thomas and William living in Hayes is well established.

Further to this link, on 25th December 1795, 1771 William, son of Ralph, married Mary Collingwood in Hayes. During the course of the next 19 years Mary gave birth to ten children, namely: 31-7-1796 Thomas, 7-1-1798 Sarah, 12-1-1800 Samuel, 21-2-1802 Matthew (died 29-12-1815), 4-12-1803 Henery (died 10-1-1806), 1805 Dinah, 12-1-1808 Charles(baptised 7-2-1808), 7-5-1809 Eliza (died19-2-1815), 28-7-1811 Geoffrey (died 11-10-1811), and 24-4-1814 William. Note that four of William and Mary's ten children died while very young. The reason for this is not in the record. It is (long-lived) 1808 Charles who was to become my great grandfather.

Unlike his forebears, William's life coincided with an extremely difficult period for the ordinary farm labourer. In the seventy years since his grandfather Thomas had moved onto the land, the population of England had nearly doubled, and this highlighted certain inefficiencies in the 'open field' system of farming. The 'cure' for this perceived agricultural problem was the enclosure of farmland to the manner we see today, but in Harmondsworth this did not occur until after William's death. However William was much affected by the general situation in the country. In the years before 1795 several bad harvests had pushed up the price of wheat. Then, to make matters worse, wars with France meant that the import of wheat from continental Europe was difficult and hence expensive. The result was that those at the bottom of the social scale needed Poor Law relief if they were not to starve, and this placed a burden on the 1601 Poor Law that it was never intended to meet. Solutions to this problem were proposed and acted upon in many parts of the country, but the one that found favour and hence was widely adopted was devised in the West Berkshire village of Speenhamland in 1795. In this system a value was placed on a 'gallon' loaf (3.8kg) which could be (say) 1s-0d. At this price level the minimum weekly wage for a single man was set to 3s-0d, for a married man 4s-6d, with 1s-6d added for each of their children. Then, as the price of a gallon loaf varied due to economic circumstances, so

From the Bottom of the Pile

the minimum wage would increase or decrease proportionately. The system was intended to be humane, but very quickly it did not work that way. Two farmers 'of substance' in a given manor would be required to contribute into the Poor Law fund in proportion to the rateable value of their land holdings. Say now that farmer 'A' paid his labourers 10s-0d a week while farmer 'B' paid his men only 8s-0d. Farmer 'A' then saw his Poor Law rate demand increase because of the low wages paid by farmer 'B' and so he reduced the wages of his labourers to 8s-0d a week. Farmer 'B' then saw his rates increase due to the action of farmer 'A' and so he reduced his wages bill accordingly. A vicious circle was established that was much to the disadvantage of the working agricultural labourer. The result was that William and his wife frequently found themselves begging for help from the Harmondsworth Poor Law fund or from the charity set up by the Dowager Countess of Uxbridge.

The record (as found) is:

From the Dowager Countess of Uxbridge Charity:
1805   William Dowden   5s-0d.
1806   William Dowden   5s-0d.

Recall that this charity was set up in 1748 to aid the 'deserving poor' who had not claimed money from the Poor Law fund during the preceding year. The charity account continued until the 1823, at which time it was closed on the grounds of its being 'irregular'. (Why? one can ask.) There were however no more Dowden entries re. this charity after 1806.

From the Churchwardens Accounts:
24-02-1800   William Dowden's wife   5s-0d.
28-02-1800   William Dowden's wife   5s-0d.
20-06-1800   William Dowden   5s-0d.
22-11-1801   William Dowden's wife   3s-0d.
23-01-1802   William Dowden   [Wife B??? (Being?) to Bed]. No sum of money noted.
28-10, 01-11, 07-11, 17-11-1802   7s-0d, 7s-0d, 3s-0d, 5s-0d respectively.
18-01-1808   William Dowden   5s-0d.

From the Vestry Minutes:
24-02-1800   Ordered that William Dowden have 5s-0d stock money. (Is this the same 5s-0d as above?)
05-03-1800   Ordered that William Dowden have 10s-6d paid by the Overseer.
24-02-1802   Dame Pearman applied for payment for nursing William Dowden's wife in laying in. Ordered to receive £1-1s-0d from Mr. Wild. ---- Remember this is a false contract by Dowden's wife.
10-03-1802   William Dowden's wife applied for Relief for her husband, ordered to receive as Mr. Wild sees needful, and desired to have one child enoculated.

William and Mary

17-11-1802	Ordered ---- William Dowden 5s-0d stock money.
01-12-1802	Ordered ---- William Dowden Rec'd of Mr. Singer Overseer 7s-0d Dowden being ill. (This record could be 17s-0d, but probably not.)
15-04-1805	Ordered, Isaac Riddington's Bill for Dowden's Children the amount £2-4s-9d. (This sum represented about one months wages for a farm labourer. It could refer to Ralph's son James and daughter Roza, or to William's children Thomas, Sarah, Samuel, Matthew and Henery. The magnitude of the sum leads the writer to believe that the children in question were those of William and (pregnant again) Mary.)

The next record of William is that of his funeral and burial in 1814. It simply reads:

11-03-1814	William Dowten aged 42 years.

Two months after the death of William his last child, a son, was born. He was named William after his father.

With the death of her husband and then the birth of her son William, Mary had two appointments at the local church. The record indicates that both these appointments were kept at a time when 12s-0d a week was the most that William could hope to earn. The costs of the burial and then the baptism are given in a table published the previous year by the then vicar. A copy of this table of fees is noted in the section named Ancestral Documents.

There are two more entries in the surviving Vestry Minutes concerning members of the Dowden family. Because at that time a wife or widow was never referred to by her own Christian name it is not possible to determine whether these records refer to Ralph's widow Kerrenhapuch, or to William's widow Mary.

30-09-1814	Ordered that 16s-0d be paid by the Overseer for Widow Dowden's Child at Chesham and that 2s-0d per week be paid by (Mr.) Ashby to be continued until further order.
27-03-1816	Ordered £1-12s-0d for clothing Dowden's Child she going into service.

By the standards we enjoy some 200 years after the lives of William, Mary and their children, they lived in very hard times. However I doubt if those in control of Poor Law operations in Harmondsworth saw matters as we would see them in our time, and the above record contains evidence in support of this.

On 23-01-1802 note was made in the Churchwardens Accounts that William's wife Mary was 'to Bed'. Clearly this means that note is made in the parish of Mary's sickness. Then on 24-02-1802 the Vestry Minutes record a claim for payment of £1-1s-0d to a Dame Pearman for nursing Mary during a period of 'laying in'. At this time a note is made "Remember this is a false contract by Dowden's wife." Within a month of the 'false contract' Mary gave birth to her son Matthew, so clearly the expectation was that Dame Pearman would be present at a birth,

From the Bottom of the Pile

and for her services she is paid a sum twice that of a fully fit labourer with a family to support. This suggests that some form of elementary health service was in operation at Harmondsworth.

On 10-03-1802 note was made in the Churchwardens Accounts that Mary 'desired to have one child enoculated'. This simple statement indicates something that to us seems incredible. During the period 1714 to 1716 while the Earl of Uxbridge was serving as Ambassador to the Sultan of Turkey, his wife noticed a local medical custom and, on her return to England, introduced it into her various manors. The medical practice was that of inoculating healthy children with live smallpox virus, and that is what Mary requested for one of her children! In 1795 Edward Jenner first inoculated people with pus from cowpox pustules in order to protect them against smallpox. His ideas worked and gradually they were adopted world-wide. But Jenner's ideas were not common practice in 1802, and at that time the normal statistic for smallpox in the European population applied. This was that 60% of the adult population caught smallpox and one third of these people died from the disease, or in other words, 20% of the adult population succumbed to smallpox. Also those that survived the disease were severely disfigured by the scarring caused by the smallpox pustules. The idea brought back to England by the Countess of Uxbridge was that children should be inoculated with live smallpox virus taken from the pustules of adult victims. Some 10% of otherwise healthy children died as a result of this procedure, but then at that time many children died when young from the multiplicity of other common diseseases. The arithmetic is easy to see, better to lose up to 10% of children through inoculation than lose 20% of these children when they were adults. In Harmondsworth the arrangement was that inoculation would be carried out by a Mr. Crouch, a 'surgeon' from Hounslow. He would inoculate the child and look after him/her during the following period of sickness. On recovery the child was returned to his/her home and Mr. Crouch was paid 3s-0d. If the child died, no payment was made. The record does not indicate which of Mary's children was inoculated, or whether the child survived. However, be that as it may, the fact that in Harmondsworth a medical measure of probable benefit in later life could be obtained using Poor Law funds again shows the existence of an elementary form of health service. (We now know that the body of the victim from whom the smallpox virus was taken was fighting the disease. This means that the potency of the virus used on the children was less than that for the population at large. For us there is perhaps one question, "Would you subject a child of yours to this procedure?")

Perhaps at this point one should summarise the nature of and the powers exercised by the Vestry Committee. All committee members were 'Messuage Holders' in the parish. That is they occupied a property that included a house, outbuildings, a courtyard and land for personal use that could contain an orchard or suchlike. In short they were the few men of substance in the parish, and their wealth was inherited from generation to generation. Thus for over 200 years in Harmondsworth we see the same surnames occurring as members of the Homage and Vestry Committee. Neither the skilled artisan nor the farm labourer could serve as a member of the Homage or Vestry Committee, and there was no form of democracy relating to decisions made.

William and Mary

Recalling decisions made that affected members of the Dowden family we see:

- Selection of those to be drafted into the Militia - e.g. Joseph in 1792. (The record states that "Joseph was drawed for the Militia", but it seems that only the poor had their names in the hat.)
- Ordering surrender to the workhouse - e.g. Ralph in 1801 when he was 67 years of age.
- Paying for midwifery - e.g. Mary in 1802.
- Paying for inoculation - e.g. William and Mary's child in 1802.
- One Committee member only (Wm. Wild) determining the extent of financial relief - e.g. for William and Mary in 1802.
- Deciding that a child will be removed from its parents and sent away from home into service - e.g. widow Kerrenhapuch and/or widow Mary's children in 1814 and 1816.

Looking again at the summary above it should be noted that there were conditions for the removal of a child from its home and being sent into service. These were that the child had to be at least seven years of age and, in the opinion of the Vestry Committee (only) its parent(s) was/were unable to support him/her. Having reached this decision, removal etc. was organised by the Overseer regardless of the feelings of the child or its parent(s). Regarding financial relief, the record clearly shows that the sums involved were at the discretion of the Vestry Committee which, in its wisdom, could delegate any given decision to one of its members. There was no such thing as 'an entitlement'. Also decisions made were part of the public record. It was not possible for a person to swindle the system by claiming relief to which he/she was not entitled.

The record notes William as being 42 years of age when he died, whereas he had an actual age of 43 years. But why did he die in early middle age? Nearly 200 years after the event, and in the absence of his body, the reason cannot be determined with any degree of certainty. However it is clear from the Poor Law record that William did not enjoy good health during his working life, and thus his environment is worthy of examination. He lived at a time in which the living standards of working people were under severe attack, and when possible he probably worked beyond reason for the sake of his family. Overwork, when coupled with a poor diet, is a well known recipe for an early demise. He could have suffered a fatal accident, although in that case one would expect there to be an appropriate comment in the church register. Lastly there is sickness as the cause of his death, and this leads to an aspect of work in which he was almost certainly involved.

William's period of work coincided with the Napoleonic wars, and before this time there were no army barracks because soldiers were billeted in the houses of the local populace. However in the Napoleonic period the army grew to a size such that the construction of barracks for accommodating men, their horses and equipment became necessary, and large barracks were established on Hounslow Heath. And of course, large numbers of soldiers and horses produce lots of waste products. Now it was during the 18th century that the value of manure for fertilising farm land became common knowledge and thus, in the Napoleonic period, two situations came together. Firstly the army wished to dispose of its biological waste products, and local farmers wished to use these products to fertilise their fields. Naturally the farmers in adjacent Heathrow were not displeased to have a 'near to hand' supply of fertiliser and hence they agreed a contract with the army for its biological waste. Writing now, without proof, it seems inevitable that William would have spent many an unhappy hour manually loading onto carts, and then spreading onto fields, both stable manure and human sewerage. It is the human sewerage aspect of the work (which undoubtably was performed by some) that brings into question the cause of William's death.

The writer's own adopted town of Woodbridge in Suffolk was also a Napoleonic garrison town, with a large barracks during this period. Now, on passing by a local cemetery, one can see a memorial to the 669 persons who died in the Woodbridge Barracks in the years 1804 to 1814. These people did not die as a result of injuries inflicted in battle, they died as a result of disease. Clearly fatal diseases were rife in the Hanoverian army and, returning to William again, I wonder about the danger to life in his (almost certain) muck spreading activities. From a technical viewpoint human sewage may contain bacterial, viral or parasitic contaminants, and if one considers bacterial contaminants only, they include botulism, cholera, dysentery and typhoid fever. It is certain that some, if not all, of the above mentioned contaminants would have been spread onto the fields at Harmondsworth courtesy the local barracks and farmers. As stated above, the cause of William's death is not known, but if it was due to sickness, was it caused by human sewage from Hounslow Heath?

Following the death of William, the gods of tragedy had not finished with his widow Mary. In February 1815 her daughter Eliza died at six years of age, then her son Matthew died at 14 years of age during the following December. The period must have been one of desperation for Mary. Perhaps, in a roundabout way, the Churchwardens accounts for Harmondsworth give a clue as to the family situation during this period. On 4th December 1822 a J??? Dowden was given 5s-0d from the above account, and then on 14th December 1823 and on 27th January 1833 a J. Dowden was given 5s-0d and 2s-0d respectively. The only known candidate for this largesse was Ralph's daughter, 1764 Jane. There is no record of a Jane Dowden in the 1841 census for Harmondsworth.

The last known record of Mary occurs in the census record of 1851. By that time Mary had remarried and was living with her son Samuel (a single man) in Harmondsworth. In the 1850's Mary would have attained the age of 80 years. Clearly she must have possessed a very strong constitution because she lived life during the most difficult of times.

Enclosure; and James

In the essays concerning William and his forebears, the agricultural system in operation in Harmondsworth was that of farming 'strips of land in large open fields'. There were also areas of land described as 'waste' or 'common', to which all residents had access for personal use. Additionally cottagers had rights in other ways, such as fishing in the manorial rivers for food. Under this system it was possible for agricultural labourers to own land under copyhold arrangements, and we know from the records that forebears such as John Guidon, Thomas Dowden and his son Ralph did so. But change was in the air during the latter part of the 18th century, and in 1819 an Enclosure Act took effect in the Manor of Harmondsworth.

In 1801, in Harmondsworth, there were 1,350 acres (540 hectares) under arable cultivation. Wheat (500 acres) and barley (450 acres) were the main crops. Peas and beans each occupied 150 acres, and some oats, rye, turnips, potatoes and rape were also grown. Slightly over one third of the parish was cultivated, and the vicar who made the above return also commented that "most of the waste land could be sown with corn to much greater advantage". This 'waste land' of about 1,300 acres was the area in which the inhabitants of Harmondsworth had, since time out of mind, right of access for the gleaning of firewood, grazing of animals etc. It was in 1805 that an 'Inclosure Act' for the parish of Harmondsworth was passed by Parliament, but no award (i.e. of land) was made at that time. An amending Act was then passed in 1816 and finally in 1819 some 1,170 acres of waste land and 1100 acres in fields and meadows were enclosed. Neither a map of land ownership for the immediate post-enclosure period nor the many sheets of paper making up the Harmondsworth Inclosure Act contain the name Dowden. It is thus certain that after the 1819 Act took effect, the Dowden family was landless. It is also certain that 1,170 acres of 'waste' land, was now in private ownership, and hence earlier (essential for life) access was now denied to the poor. Clearly the 1819 Harmondsworth Inclosure Act was a disaster for the Dowden family.

The above paragraph contains recorded 'facts' as they apply to Harmondsworth, however Enclosure Acts, on a nationwide basis, contained side-effects that are not, individually, in the record. Many of these side-effects would have had an impact on the Dowden family in Heathrow/Harmondsworth. Many poor cottagers who kept a cow or a few geese on the waste land, and who used it also for their supply of fuel, were tenants of the cottages in which they lived. In this context it seems certain that William's heir would have been a tenant and not a copyholder of his cottage in 1819. When enclosure took place the owner of rented cottages received an allotment of land as compensation for the extinction of earlier rights on the waste or common land. The tenant got nothing. Nor, as generally recorded, were the rents for these cottages reduced. Suppose now that William's heir was regarded as the copyholder of the family cottage. Could he prove this by way of documentation to the Commisioner who was overseeing the land ownership changes imposed by the Enclosure Act? If not, he also lost his earlier common rights without compensation. Consider now the owner of a few small plots of land under the strip cultivation system. Under an Enclosure Act he would receive a small parcel of land of (say) equivalent acreage. But he was now required to fence his land, and this was often either uneconomic or beyond his financial resources. His only solution was to sell to his more prosperous neighbour the title to his land, but of course at minimum price because the neighbour knew he had no choice in the matter.

In summary, the previous land arrangement whereby peasants generally had a land holding was replaced by one of large landowners and a landless labouring force without their earlier rights that dated back to Saxon times. In simple language, it was robbery by those in power.

In 1819 the Dowden family living at Heathrow could have included one or more of Ralph's daughters by his first marriage. The ladies in question were 1759 Elizabeth, 1762 Mary and 1764 Jane. A later record leads to the expectation that 1764 Jane did not marry and hence could well have continued to live in her father's home. Looking now at others related to Heathrow, there were Ralph's widow Kerrenhapuch with her children - 1799 James, 1802 Roza and 1806 Phillis, and also William's widow Mary with her surviving children -1796 Thomas, 1798 Sarah, 1805 Dinah, 1808 Charles, and 1814 William. But the record shows that in 1814 and 1816 two Dowden children were removed by the overseer to work as servants elsewhere and hence they would not have been at Heathrow in 1819. Sadly these children were not named. Therefore at the time of enclosure, Ralph's daughter 1762 Mary may have been living at Heathrow. Ralph's widow Kerrenhapuch and William's Mary, together with their younger or female children, were living at Heathrow in 1819, but there is no record for 1819 that gives information on 1796 Thomas and 1799 James. Later records show that 1796 Thomas survived to marry and have his own family but was he living at Heathrow in 1819? We do not know. Coming now to 1799 James the facts are known, and these are given below in all their detail. However before reading the records concerning James, the reader is asked to peruse the above notes on enclosure in order to imagine the living conditions following the events of 1819 as they applied to a landless family comprising one or two labourers, perhaps an elderly spinster, two widows and four dependent children. The plight of the Dowden's must have been desperate.

Returning now to recorded facts, it is against the above background that James, son of Ralph and now twenty years of age, decided in early February 1820 to ease his financial burden by stealing some poultry. The following information is now taken from the Old Bailey record. The owner of the birds, a James Morris of Harlington, claimed he saw his poultry at 6-00 pm on 9th February, and by 6-00 am the following morning they had gone. The birds in question were six tame ducks and a tame drake kept in an outhouse, and four tame geese and a tame gander kept in a geese house. The court valued the ducks and drake at 2s-0d (10p) each, the geese at 3s-6d (17.5p) each and the gander at 5s-0d (25p), giving a total of £1 13s-0d (£1-65p). James Morris expressed the view that their value was £10-0s-0d as they were kept for breeding. The evidence of witnesses clearly showed that James arrived, with the birds, in the Leadenhall Market in the City of London at between 9-00 am and 10-00 am on 10th February. (James must have travelled

Enclosure; and James

overnight with a cart containing live ducks and geese. How did he manage the initial part of this exercise without waking anyone?) Meanwhile James Morris must have had a good idea as to the fate of his birds because he travelled to the Leadenhall Market, arriving at about 10-15 am. (James Morris saw his poultry was missing at about 6-00 am. It takes time to saddle a horse etc., and he travelled the 17 miles to the City of London by 10-15 am. He must have been in a hurry!) At this time the birds were in the possession of a poulterer, all dead, but awkwardly killed, and one was still warm. Suffice it to say that 'beyond reasonable doubt' James was guilty of their theft and sale. There is no evidence regarding a possible accomplice.

It is of interest to note that James Morris must have quickly left the market and returned home. The involvement of James Dowden was then made known to the local constable who said he went some five or six times to the defendants house, but did not see him. An independent witness at court testified that James was seen coming home at between 4-00 pm and 5-00 pm in the afternoon of 10th February. In practice James was not apprehended until a fortnight later. The poulterer was also arrested, presumably for the purchase of stolen goods, but there is no record of his being prosecuted for his part in James' activities.

The crime was committed on 10th February 1820, and James' trial was held on the following 12th April. He was found guilty and sentenced to seven years transportation to Australia. After sentence James was held in 'prison hulk' accommodation prior to sailing into exile. He was then transferred to a 430 tons vessel named Hebe, which left Portsmouth on 31st July 1820 and arrived in Sydney Cove on 30th December 1820. There were 30 convicts on board the Hebe and all survived the passage. The convicts were all male, four were teenagers, and with one exception the remainder were all under 40 years of age. The sentences were either transportation for seven years, fourteen years, or for life. The teenagers (youngest 16 years of age) all received a life sentence.

The first Australian mention of James is dated 28th January 1822. On this date he was charged with 'neglect of work and insolence to his overseer'. The magistrates court at Parramatta found him guilty and sentenced James to 50 lashes and return to his gang at Longbottom Farm. Clearly James was not cowed into submission by having the skin on his back cut to ribbons, and in February 1822 he absconded from his place of work/detention. Now this was a very serious step to take because at this time a European fugitive could not live off the land, and the local Aboriginal population would not co-operate in keeping him 'free'. In short, an absconder could only survive by criminal activity. On 21st February James committed a burglary and also at about that time he committed a highway robbery. Using the words contained in Government papers of the time, James had become a 'notorious bushranger'.

With James unable to travel far from the Sydney area it followed that his location would be noticed by a white inhabitant, and in this case he was seen by a John Hinns. According to the record this John approached a local official suggesting that he (John) could gain a preferment if he informed the authorities on the whereabouts of James. John Hinns was then advised

From the Bottom of the Pile

that such a preferment would be requested if James was captured, but that the reverse would be the case if he was not both found and captured. But James was found and captured. The consequence was that in a court on 18th June 1822 James pleaded guilty to a charge of felony and was sentenced to death. The sentence was carried out on 5th July 1822, and thus died a relative of the writer at 22 years of age.

Strangely perhaps the hanging was not the last mention of James. On 29th July 1822 a letter was written by an official to the Colonial Secretary asking for John Hinns to be given preferment. By August a Stephen Curran, who was one of those active in apprehending James, could not find work. He asked for help, and again a letter was sent 'up the line'. The words used in this letter were, "Can't find work as Active Service rendered to the Crown makes him obnoxious to the public in general and precludes him from finding any kind of labour". He was, "Directed to apply to the Chief Engineer as the only office likely to employ him". In November 1822 a John Slater used his involvement in the capture of James as the reason for requesting a conditional pardon. It appears to have been granted, and John Slater was joined by his wife and four children. Following the death of John Slater in 1824, his part in the apprehension of James was used to obtain a grant of land for his widow.

Great grandfather Charles was born in 1808 and hence would have known James. After his marriage in 1836, Charles named one of his children James and another James Henry. There was only one James Dowden from a previous generation that Charles could have known. Did Charles remember James as an antisocial villain or as a victim of his times? We will never know.

Charles, Ellen and their Children

Charles, son of William and Mary was born in 1808 and spent his long life living at Heathrow. He was born when the 'strip' method of cultivation was the norm, but spent his working life after the Harmondsworth Enclosure Act of 1819. Clearly he was eleven years of age when the Enclosure Act was passed, and hence was a youth during the particularly hard time that working people endured during the early 1820's. The forebears of Charles (William excepted?) could be described as peasants who owned small areas of land and had access to waste land of over 1000 acres for grazing and firewood. Charles had nothing. He was simply an illiterate agricultural labourer.

Noted in the essay on William, the 1801 record shows that up to that date the farm land in Harmondsworth was used mainly for the growing of grain. This changed during the course of 19th century. In earlier times the fruit and vegetables consumed by those living in London were grown mainly in nearby villages such as Fulham. However during the 19th century London expanded, and land in villages such as Fulham was used for manufacturing, the building of houses, and associated infrastructure. The result was that land in outlying areas such as Harmondsworth became used for market garden crops and orchards as opposed to the grain of earlier times. In Harmondsworth in 1839 there were 100 acres of orchards and three market gardens (area not known). In the 1860's there were over 240 acres of orchards and this area increased with time. It is clear that during his working life Charles was subjected to changes in farming practices unknown to his forebears.

There are two records only for the 'dark' period in the 1820's. The first is the marriage of Ralph's daughter Roza (now called Rose) to a Zebalon Lipscombe on 24th December 1821. The second is the death of in 1825 of Joseph, son of 1731 John and uncle of Charles. Joseph was the man who was conscripted into the militia during the Napoleonic period. Then we see that Zebalon and Rose did not have an easy start to their married life. The Churchwardens accounts show that Zebalon received from the Poor Law fund 7s-6d + 7s-6d + 10s-0d in the years 1831, 1832 and 1840 respectively. The 1840 payment is of interest in that the 1834 Poor Law Act all but forbade the giving of financial assistance to the poor unless they were first incarcerated in the workhouse. However in the 1841 census Zebalon and Rose share the same house, from which it is inferred that the full impact of the 1834 Act was not imposed upon Zebalon.

On 27th December 1836 Charles married an Ellen Finning at Christchurch, Ealing. At the time of the wedding the ages of Charles and Ellen were 28 years and 18 years respectively. Later records show that Ellen was born in Ireland, however no record has been found indicating her place of birth or anything relating to her forebears. During the next 26 years Charles and Ellen had twelve children. These were: 20-9-1837 Henry, 14-7-1838 Mary Ann, 22-6-1840 William, 22-5-1842 Thomas, 1844 James, 1847 Dinah, 1849 Anne, 3-12-1851 Charles, 1854 Ellen, 1857 James Henry, 1859 George Henry, and finally my grandfather 1862 Joseph. It is recorded that 1837 Henry died shortly after birth and that a James and Dinah Dowden died in the fourth quarter of 1848. The 1848 record does not indicate the parentage of James and Dinah, but it seems safe to assume that they were the children of Charles and Ellen because their names are not noted as part of the Dowden household in the 1851 census.

In the 1830's the average wage of agricultural labourers in the Harmondsworth area was 12s-0d a week. This figure is considerably more than that of earlier days, but of course its actual value depended on the 1830's cost of living. It is also recorded that there were reports of discontent in the area at this time, so it seems reasonable to presume that the average wage was considered inadequate when compared with the cost of living. Set against the above is the 1834 Poor Law Amendment Act. This amended parts of the 1601 Poor Law Act because social conditions were far removed from those that existed in late Elizabethan times. One of the main aims of the amendment was to reduce the increasing cost of maintaining the fit, but otherwise unemployed poor. Specifically the new Act stated:

- No able-bodied person was to receive money or other help from the Poor Law authorities except in a workhouse;
- Conditions in workhouses were to be made very harsh to discourage people from wanting to receive help;
- Workhouses were to be built in every parish or, if parishes were too small, in unions of parishes; (There was at this time a workhouse in the Harmondsworth area.)
- Ratepayers in each parish or union had to elect a Board of Guardians to supervise the workhouse, to collect the Poor Rate and to send reports to Central Poor Law Commission.
- The three man Central Poor Law Commission would be appointed by the government and would be responsible for supervising the Amendment Act throughout the country.

Returning to Charles, the record indicates that he received moneys from the Poor Law fund on a reasonably regular basis. The sums in question were: 4s-0d in 1842, 2s-0d + 5s-0d in 1844, 5s-0d + 5s-0d in 1846 and in 1847, 5s-0d + 10s-0d + 10s-0d in 1848, 5s-0d + 5s-0d in 1851, and 5s-0d in 1852. In 1854 Charles received 10s-0d because of his wife's confinement, and in 1855 he received 5s-0d because three of his children were ill. He then received two times 10s-0d in each of 1862 and 1863 without reasons being given. With the exception of 1854, 1862 and 1863 the payments to Charles were all made in the December to February period. Perhaps this indicates that support for at least some of the agricultural labourers in the parish was normal in the winter months. However, be that as it may, given the Poor Law conditions noted as (i) and (ii) above did Charles spend part of the winter periods in the local workhouse? Sadly, records on this matter have not been located. Sadly also, 1863 is the last year for which the churchwardens accounts have been located and thus it is not known if Charles received Poor Law relief in later years.

However for Charles, poverty in the early 1860's was probably the least of his problems. His wife Ellen died on 12th April 1864. The death certificate gives the cause of death as: "Softening of Brain - Shock from Burning of Body". Ellen was just 45 years of age. Medical advice indicates that in the case of severe burning, the blood supply is directed to the wounds and hence the brain is starved of oxygen. Poor Ellen will have suffered dizziness and confusion before losing consciousness and then her life. As to why she was burned, there is probably a simple answer. At that time ladies wore long dresses and all cooking was done on an open fireplace. With soap as an expensive commodity it would be normal for a lady's working dress to be contaminated with fat, and hence the danger of setting light to a dress. Also, Ellen may have been 'clumsy' due to being pregnant at the time. In any event, in 1864, Ellen died leaving a widower and eight children.

Charles was born in 1808 and he died in 1891. In the year 1851 he was in his mid-life, and perhaps it is of interest to look at the environment in which he lived, compared with that some 150 years earlier, and later. In about the year 1700 the inhabitants in a village were largely self-sufficient. At that time the Manor of Harmondsworth contained just over 100 houses whose occupants were liable to pay Window Tax. The inference is that the population of the Manor would have been about 800, with 150 persons being of adult age. Also, in 1700, the population of the UK was about 5,000,000. In 1851 the population of the UK had risen to about 19,000,000, that of the Harmondsworth area to 1308 persons, with the majority of the 'heads of household' being agricultural labourers. However by 1851, although the village of Harmondsworth was still largely self-sufficient its inhabitants were not. (Note here that the agricultural labourer was now landless.) The 1851 census for Harmondsworth indicates the extent to which the 'producing people' were served by others in supporting trades. The figures were:

5 Bakers	1 Basket Maker	5 Blacksmiths	3 Butchers
1 Bricklayer	3 Carpenters	4 Dressmakers	3 Grocers
1 Hatter	8 Hay-dealers	1 Inn Keeper	2 Laundress'
1 Licensed Victualler	2 Painters	4 Police Constables	6 Publicans
1 Salesman	School Mistress	2 Shepherds	3 Shoemakers
1 Stay-maker	1 Tax Collector	4 Wheelwrights	

In the year 2000 Heathrow is an international airport and hence no sensible population comparisons for the parish of Harmondsworth can be made. However both present-day common sense and a visit to the area shows that the host of tradespeople noted above no longer exist in the area. Society has completed a 'local' process in that neither the village nor its inhabitants are now self-sufficient. (As an aside, the nation is no longer self-sufficient - but this is not a subject for this family history.)

In order to keep itself informed on the size of the UK population, the government of the day organised a census in the year 1801 and arranged that successive censuses would be taken in April at ten years intervals. The returns for 1801 to 1831 give information on numbers only, but those from 1841 on give family details. The 1841 returns for Harmondsworth and Harlington include the following:

From the Bottom of the Pile

Harmondsworth

Philip Burgess	52 years	
Mary Burgess	68 years	Widow of William Dowden
Zebalon Lipscombe	45 years	
Roseanna Lipscombe	40 years	Daughter of Ralph and Kerrenhapuch Dowden
Susan Lipscombe	17 years	
Elizabeth Lipscombe	14 years	
Emelia Lipscombe	7 years	
Ann Lipscombe	5 years	
Hannah Lipscombe	3 years	
Josiah Lipscombe	1 year	
Charles Dowden	33 years	Great grandfather of writer, son of William.
Alen Dowden	25 years	Great grandmother.
Mary A. Dowden	3 years	(Baptised as Marianne.)
William Dowden	17 months	
Alen Lipscombe	10 years	Daughter of Zebalon and Rose(anna).

Harlington

William Dowden	27 years	Youngest son of William.
Amelia Dowden	29 years	
Sarah Dowden	3 years	
Martha Dowden	-1 year	(Born in 1842.)

The 1841 census shows the remarriage of Mary, William's widow, to a younger man. Such remarriages were not uncommon at the time. Also there must have been a close relationship between Charles and his half-aunt Rose(anna); and perhaps by accommodating his cousin Alen he saved her from forcible removal from the parish by the Overseer. 1814 William is shown as a married man in nearby Harlington, his son 1852 William was working in London 40+ years later.

Charles, Ellen and their Children

Collating the Harmondsworth census records for the 19th century we see:

1841			**1851**			**1861**		
Charles Dowden	33		Charles Dowden	42		Charles Dowden	56	
Alen Dowden	25		Ellen Dowden	32		Ellen Dowden	40	
Mary Dowden	3		William Dowden	10		Thomas Dowden	19	
William Dowden	17m		Thomas Dowden	8		Ann Dowden	12	
Alen Lipscombe	10		Ann Dowden	1		Charles Dowden	9	
			Ellen Dowden	7				
Philip Burgess	52		Philip Burgess	61		James Dowden	5	
Mary Burgess	68		Mary Burgess	79		George Dowden	2	
			Samuel Dowden (son of Mary)	51				
			Mary A. Dowden (servant of Samuel Hunt)	12		Mary A. Dowden (servant of Richard Weekly)	22	

1871			**1881**			**1891**		
Charles Dowden	65		Charles Dowden	26		Charles Dowden	38	
Charles Dowden	20		Jane Dowden	26		Jane Dowden	35	
Ellen Dowden	17		Charles Dowden	6m		Charles H. Dowden	10	
George Dowden	11		Charles Dowden	74		Nellie Dowden	9	
Joseph Dowden	8		George Dowden	23		William W. Dowden	6	
						George H. Dowden	4	
						Lily J. Dowden	1	
Mary A. Dowden (general servant of Richard Weekly)	31		Mary A. Dowden (servant of Elizabeth Weekly widow of Richard)	42		Mary A. Dowden (servant of Elizabeth Weekly 69 years)	49	

At the time of the above investigation the 1901 census was not in the public domain.

One might think that in having censuses taken every ten years, the ages of those included would be noted as having ages also at ten years intervals. It would seem that our 19th century forebears had little interest in their exact ages. 1808 Charles remained as head of the household until the 1871 census. Then, some time between 1871 and 1881 his son, 1851 Charles, marries and

49

becomes head of the household. Did 1808 Charles retire at (say) 70 years of age? No details on this have been found in the record. Charles died on 6th March 1891 at the reported age of 84 years. The cause of death was given as "Old Age, Exhaustion". Between 1871 and 1881 daughter Ellen disappears from the record. Her fate is not known. By 1891, George Henry (born 1859) was married and living at The Moor in nearby Stanwell. He was noted as a Farm Carter in the 1891 census.

In the 1841 census returns given above, 1814 William is noted as 27 years of age and married to Amelia aged 29 years. Successive censuses show that over the years they remained in Harlington and had five children. The 1881 census then shows William and Amelia living alone together, their children presumably having 'flown the nest'. Then, in 1891 the census shows the following for one house: George Lockey 65, Dinah Lockey 85, William Dowden 77. Now this Dinah Lockey is exactly the right age for 1805 Dinah Dowden, sister of both 1814 William and great grandfather Charles. For whatever reason, Dinah married a much younger man, and this brings to mind the action of 1771 William's widow Mary in marrying Philip Burgess. It also shows how, in old age, it was not unknown for siblings to join each other in mutual support. William died in 1894 aged 79 years, and Dinah outlived them all, finally capitulating in 1899 at 93 years of age. Finally 1800 Samuel Dowden is shown in the 1871 census as being 75 years of age and living in Harlington as a lodger with a Thomas and Jane Wilkinson. Samuel died in 1880 at 79 years of age. There is no known record indicating that Samuel was ever married.

The first narrative relating to the lives of the children of Charles and Ellen concerns 1838 Mary Ann. In this, the dated statements are taken from the public record, but others are from Dowden family history verbally given to the writer by a living (1990's) William Wild. As noted above, in 1851 Mary Ann was a servant to a local farmer of 470 acres named Samuel Hunt. By our standards it is remarkable that a girl of only twelve years of age should be living away from home as someone's servant. Then, in the 1861 and later census returns, she was a servant in the employ of the Weekly family. Now reference back to 16th century, and later records, indicate a succession of people named Wild (usually William) who were significant farmers in the Manor of Harmondsworth. The same records, from about 1700 on, indicate the presence in the manor of a family named Weekly, and this family formed a part of the local squirearchy. Also the Wild's and the Weekly's were non-conformists who, over the generations, had intermarried. Proof of their non-conformity over this long period can be found in church records that do not include their baptisms, but do include, as required by law, their burials. (Often in privileged church locations.) The Richard Weekly, who had employed Mary Ann by 1861, was the last of his line and following family tradition he was a member of the local Baptist Chapel. He was also partly disabled, and his disability was such that he was known as 'Shaky Weekly'; the condition apparently being caused by his being very close to a lightning strike when he was young. In any event, with Richard, 200 years of Weekly squires in the manor came to an end because he and his wife suffered from an inability to have children. This left Mary Ann, and perhaps others, looking after the needs of only two people in the large Weekly house near to the Zoar (later Zion) Baptist Chapel in Longford. In the period 1871 to 1881 Richard Weekly died and Mary

Charles, Ellen and their Children

Ann remained with his widow Elizabeth as her personal servant. Further to this, the present (1990's) William Wild told me that Mary Ann was regarded as being Elizabeth's companion, a position of dignity compared with that of a mere servant. Then on 2nd January 1899 Elizabeth Weekly died at 77 years of age. The newspaper reporting her death noted "The deceased's own servant would also have been numbered among the mourners, but was prevented by indisposition." Clearly Mary Ann had a place of dignity within 'the Weekly family', but whose family now that the Weekly's had died out? As mentioned above, over many generations there had been intermarriage between members of the Weekly and Wild families, with the result that a major part of the Richard and Elizabeth's estate was willed to the Wild family. From a conversation with William Wild it seems clear that the new Wild owner of the Weekly estate felt that he had a duty of care towards Mary Ann. Fortunately perhaps, the Weekly estate included a four-roomed cottage, one of a pair, built in the 1850's by Richard Weekly as an appendage to his Zoar Baptist Chapel. This property was, in essence, just across the road from the Weekly house and the new Wild owner established Mary Ann as a tenant in this cottage.

Mary Ann spent the remainder of her life in Zion Cottage as it is now called. In 1903 she married a William Bampton, a member of the Baptist Church, and six years later, on 18th September 1909 she died in her cottage. Her body is buried in the cemetery attached to St. Mary's Church Harmondsworth. Hers is the only grave of a 19th century, and earlier, Dowden that can be identified from a headstone in the St. Mary's Church cemetery. Personally writing (as Mary-Ann's great nephew), seeing her plot and headstone has helped to bring the tale of the Harmondsworth Dowden's to life. May she rest in peace. Mary Ann's funeral details were published and she was described as a very popular person. Noted among the mourners were "T., W., C., and G. Dowden's and their wives". If the initials refer to Mary Ann's brothers, as is possible, then they refer to 1842 Thomas, 1840 William, 1859 George Henry and 1851 Charles.

Following the death of Charles' wife Ellen in 1864 it must have been 1849 Anne who was given a major responsibility for keeping house and home together. Sadly there are no known records of the fate of the Dowden family in the immediate post-1864 period. However in the late 1860's Anne met a young chimney sweep from London named John Thomas Scott and on 27th February 1870 they were married in St. Mary's Church Harmondsworth. Anne then left Harmondsworth to join her husband in London. It seems probable that Anne will have met an almost unknown world when she moved to London. In 1870, in Heathrow, Anne will have used an outside privy which was simply a hole in the ground with some sort of seating arrangement, lighting by candles at night was the norm, drinking water was obtained from a well or pond, and she had the cosy arrangement of living in a two-bedroomed cottage with her father, one sister, and four brothers of varying ages. Perhaps Anne and younger sister Ellen alone were given the second bedroom, but who knows? In London, Anne would have enjoyed the use of an outside toilet connected to a sewerage system, gas lighting, a mains water supply, and a bed with her husband. What could be better? Shortly after her marriage Anne was joined by her younger brother 1857 James Henry. From later records we see that James was learning the trade of chimney sweeping from his brother in law, John. The next record of Anne occurs

From the Bottom of the Pile

in the 1881 census when we see the following:

1881 Chelsea

John Scott	31 years	Head	M	Chimney Sweep	
Annie Scott	31 years	Wife	M		Born at Heathrow
Lilley Scott	10 years	Dau	U		
John Scott	9 years	Son	U		
Walter Scott	8 years	Son	U		
Joseph Dowden	17 years	Servant		Chimney Sweep	Born at Heathrow

(M = married, U = unmarried.)

It can be seen above, that in 1881 James Henry was no longer living with John, (as shown below he was an independent chimney sweep in 1881), and that 1862 Joseph was now learning the chimney sweeping trade. At this time John, Ann and family were living at 60, Pavilion Road, Chelsea. Also at this address was living a Hignett family of four persons and also a lodger. A late 20th century look at 60, Pavilion Road leads one to believe that it could only accommodate the Scott family with difficulty. The house must have been 'cosy' to say the least, but then such were the living conditions in working class homes at that time. In a search of the 1891 census no record has been found of John and Anne in Chelsea. In practice the Old Library in Chelsea stores the late 19th century lists of people on the electoral role. It appears that there is no record of a John Scott who could conceivably be the husband of Anne in these documents. The conclusion is that either John and Anne had moved away, which seems unlikely due to the chimney sweeping 'round' or that John had died, with Anne and her growing family having moved elsewhere. Now Anne, if still alive in 1891, had moved from Chelsea, and there is no known record of a return to Harmondsworth.

The later history of 1851 Charles is partly known due to meeting one of his granddaughters in the 1990's. 1851 Charles married a Jane Manders in about 1879 and they had nine surviving children in the period 1880 to 1903. Their eldest son 1880 Charles Henry joined the army as a boy entrant, and rose through the ranks to become a commissioned officer. During the 1914 to 1918 war he gained the temporary rank of Brigadier General and eventually retired with the rank of Major. He was the first known Dowden to climb out of the conditions of poverty endured by his known forebears. He is remembered by his branch of the family as being the owner of a large imposing house in Richmond. By way of contrast his youngest brother, 1903 John Thomas, served in the army as a Private and was killed as were many, during the 1914-1918 war.

As mentioned above, 1857 James Henry left Harmondsworth in 1870-71 to live in London with his sister 1849 Anne and her chimney sweep husband John Scott. The plan was that James would learn the trade of chimney sweeping, and in that he was successful. It is not known for how long James remained with John Scott at 60, Pavilion Road Chelsea, but in 1881 we see the following census record:

James Dowden	24 years	Head	M	Chimney Sweep	Born at Heathrow
Lily Dowden	21 years	Wife	M		
Lily Dowden	8 months		U		

All resident at Lute Street, Chelsea. (M = married, U = unmarried.)

Clearly in 1881 James had left the home of John Scott, and he may have been in the process of establishing his own business.

In 1891 we see the following census record from Chelsea:

James Dowden	34 years	Head	M	Chimney Sweep	Born at Heathrow
Lily Dowden	31 years	Wife	M		Born at Pimlico
James Dowden	9 years	Son	U		Born at Hammersmith

In this record James is not noted as being either an employer or an employee. This means that he was self-employed at this time. Also it is seems ominous that young Lily is not mentioned in this census return.

Thanks to an investigation in Fulham Archives Department much is known about James and his chimney sweeping business. James established a one-man business in the Walham Green (now Fulham Broadway) area and spent the remainder of his working life in that location. By coincidence my maternal grandparents lived less than a mile from Walham Green, and my maternal uncle's childhood memory was that when in his locality a chimney needed sweeping, the cry was, "send for the Dowden's". Newspaper articles indicate that James started his chimney sweeping business in Knightsbridge before moving to Fulham in the late 19th century. This may have relevance in terms of the absence of John Scott et. al. from the 1891 census. In these articles James junior is noted as joining his father's business at 10 years of age -- going to school for an hour a day at the same time. The photograph in the Ancestral Documents section is of 1857 James and his son. James senior carried on his business in Fulham until about the end of the 1914-18 war when he retired to Slough.

After the retirement of his father, James junior continued in the business until his own eventual retirement on the grounds of ill-health in 1951. Despite his ill-health he had a long retirement, dying in October 1966 at 84 years of age. During his life James junior was married and had two daughters, and they in their turn were also married. A son-in-law of James junior continued the business until the introduction of smokeless zones in London. In 1968 one, or maybe both, of the granddaughters of 1857 James felt that they should leave a record for posterity by telling the tale of their grandfather, 1857 James. The tale is in the Fulham Archives. In this tale they recall how grandfather Dowden was one of the last 'chimney boys' before this harsh practice was prohibited by law. They also recorded how James showed the scars on his elbows and arms to provide evidence of his early experiences. A 1976 publication then records that: "Grandfather Dowden scuttled up and down chimneys in the 1830's as a climbing boy, "But," says (grandson-

From the Bottom of the Pile

in-law) Jack cheerfully, "Lord Shaftesbury put an end to all that in 1840". Now it would be improper to suggest that 1857 James was never required by John Scott to climb up chimneys in a manner forbidden by law. But he could not have done this in the 1830's and hence have been relieved by the passing of an 1840 Act of Parliament. But is this tale of exaggeration worth telling? Perhaps, if for only one reason. On reading the above 'false tale' the Fulham archivist was informed of the error and also of the fact that her own census records in the archive proved the point. She made it abundantly clear that she was not in the least interested in either checking the census or inserting a relevant comment into the file containing the 'history' of 1857 James. Neither had she any interest in accepting a 'corrective statement' from a third party. Anyone now reading this archive, without also searching age records, will be misled. In the writers view the archivist in question was not fit for purpose. However I suspect that one statement made by a granddaughter of 1857 James can be taken as the truth. She recalled how, "When her husband had earned good money he would go along the street waving a leg of lamb". Clearly he didn't get rich by sweeping chimneys.

By 1891 George Henry, born 1859, was married and living at The Moor in nearby Stanwell. George was noted as a Farm Carter and his family situation was: George H. Dowden 30 years, Rosa Y. 28 years, Florence J. 6 years, Ada E. 5 years, George C. 2 years and Joseph R. 9 months. No more is known about George and his family. There is however an item of speculation on which the truth is not known. 1859 George was the elder brother of the writer's grandfather, 1862 Joseph. After their respective marriages George named his second son Joseph, and Joseph named his eldest son George. Was this a coincidence one can ask, and to that question there is no certain answer. However it is not possible for the writer to note the above 'naming' facts without an uneasy feeling concerning events in the early 20th century.

As noted, last of the children of Charles and Ellen was my grandfather, 1862 Joseph. The narrative on his life is given in the next essay.

Joseph, Jessie and their Children

As noted in the essay on Charles and his children, Joseph was born in Heathrow in 1862 and he was to become the writer's grandfather. When Joseph was only two years age his mother died as a result of being badly burned, and this probably meant that his elder sisters 1849 Anne and 1854 Ellen played a significant role in his early upbringing. Nothing is known of Joseph's early life, other than that he was living at Heathrow in the family home. In 1870 his sister Anne married a chimney sweep named John Scott, and Anne then moved from Heathrow to Chelsea. Very shortly afterwards, 1857 James followed his sister to Chelsea and, under the tutelage of John Scott, he learned the trade of chimney sweeping. Then, by 1881, Joseph was living with John and Anne, and Joseph was also practicing the trade of chimney sweeping. From the viewpoint of the writer's direct forebears, Joseph was the first to leave Heathrow since 1725, and the first to leave Harmondsworth since 1630.

Before noting the narrative concerning Joseph, it is appropriate to repeat the words of a social commentator of the time on the working classes in London during the 1850's. The man in question was Henry Mayhew. He wrote specifically about working class life in the east end of London but his words are relevant to all of London, and (in the 1990's) his book is still in print. Relevant quotations are:

"There are many reasons why the chimney-sweepers have ever been a distinct and peculiar class. They have long been looked down upon as the lowest order of workers, and treated with contumely (contempt) by those who were but little better themselves. The peculiar nature of their work giving them not only a filthy appearance, but an offensive smell, of itself, in a manner, prohibited them from associating with other working men; and the natural effect of such proscription has been to compel them to herd together apart from others, and acquire habits and peculiarities of their own widely differing from the characteristics of the rest of the labouring classes. - - - - - Notwithstanding the disrepute in which sweepers have ever been held, there are many classes of workers beneath them in intelligence. - - - - - The great mass of the agricultural labourers are known to be almost as ignorant as the beasts they drive; but sweepers, from whatever cause it may arise, are known, in many instances, to be shrewd, intelligent and active. - - - - - The chimney sweepers generally are fond of drink; indeed their calling, like that of dustmen, is one of those that naturally lead to it. The men declare that they are ordered to drink gin and smoke as much as they can, in order to rid the stomach of the soot they may have swallowed during their work. - - - - - The sweepers in general are, I am assured, fond of oleaginous food; fat broth, fagots, and what is often called 'greasy' meat. - - - - - They are considered a short-lived people, and among the journeymen, the masters 'on their own hook', &c., few old men are to be met with. Many of these men still suffer, I am told, from the chimney sweepers cancer, which is said to arise mainly from unclean habits. Some sweepers assure me that they have vomitted balls of soot." [Further to Mayhew: Fresh soot is an active carcinogen. Without the availability of efficient face masks, breathing soot into the lungs requires no further comment. In 19th century sweepers soot also found its way into the 'sweaty crutch' areas and, with lack of adequate bathing facilities, cancer of the testicles was a common cause of death among chimney sweepers.]

Returning to 1881 we see from the census that Joseph was 19 years of age and living in with his sister and family in 60, Pavilion Road, Chelsea. At the same time there was a Gorton family with an adolescent daughter living at 111, Boston Place, Marylebone. Both census records are noted below.

1881 Chelsea

John Scott	31 years	Head	M	Chimney Sweep	
Annie Scott	31 years	Wife	M		Born at Heathrow
Lilley Scott	10 years	Dau	U		
John Scott	9 years	Son	U		
Walter Scott	8 years	Son	U		
Joseph Dowden	17 years	Servant	U	Chimney Sweep	Born at Heathrow

Also a Hignett family of four and a lodger.

1881 Marylebone

Joseph Gorton	48 years	Head	M	Carman	Born at Marylebone
Annie Gorton	47 years	Wife	M	Laundress	" " " " " " "
Alice Hards	21 years	Dau	M	Laundress	" " " " " " "
Joseph Gorton	18 years	Son	U	Carman	" " " " " " "
Jessie Gorton	13 years	Dau	U		" " " " " " "
William Gorton	11 years	Son	U		" " " " " " "
Benjamin Withenden	52 years	Br-L	U	Newsagent	" " " " " " "
Daisy Hards	16 mths	G-Da	U		Born at Paddington

Clearly the maiden name of of Annie Gorton was Withenden. The 1881 census return indicates that no other people with the surname Withenden were present in London/Middlesex at that time.

Moving on to 1887, Joseph Dowden, the writer's future grandfather, had left his sister's home in Chelsea and was living at 6, Circus Street Marylebone. At that time Circus Street was situated between the south side of Marylebone Road and Upper York Street, and census information shows that it contained a number of common lodging houses that were occupied by many tenants. These houses in Circus Street have since been demolished, replacement properties have been built, and the road is now named Enford Street, W.1. Boston Place, the home of the Gorton family is still in existence (1990's) and it is located on the northern side of Marylebone Road. The home locations of Joseph Dowden and Jessie Gorton were separated by only about 300 metres.

Joseph, Jessie and their Children

Also in 1887, Annie Gorton is described as a laundry manageress, and her daughter Jessie now 19-20 years of age, was working as a laundress. With chimney sweep Joseph living in a multi-occupation residence it seems probable that he was in frequent need of laundry services and presumably the Gorton family enjoyed his patronage. However it was not the convenience of a nearby laundry, nor the washing abilities of its staff, that proved to be the most attractive part of the establishment. Suffice it to state that Joseph Dowden and Jessie Gorton were married on the 23rd. August 1887 at St. Mary's Church in the Parish of Marylebone.

At the time of writing (1990's at this point in the narrative) the latest census return in the public domain is that of 1891. Noted overleaf is the return for Joseph and his family.

1891 St. Geo. Hanover Square

Joseph Dowden	27 years	Head	M	Chimney Sweep	Born at Heathrow
Jessie Dowden	24 years	Wife	M		Born at Marylebone
George Dowden	3 years	Son	U		" " " " " " "
Albert Dowden	1 year	Son	U		Born at Chelsea.

Also in the 1891 census records the employment status of people in work was noted. Joseph was noted as an employee, but of whom is not indicated. Meanwhile, Joseph's brother James is not noted as either an employer or an employee, so he was self-employed. Thus James was not Joseph's employer. Sister Anne with her husband John do not appear in the 1891 record, and hence Joseph would not have been employed by his brother-in-law. The fate of Ann and her husband John is unknown,

We see from the 1891 census that Joseph and Jessie had two children and that they were living at 11, Grosvenor Cottages, Whittaker Street, Pimlico, London S.W. In the course of the next eleven years they had four more children, and when the writer's father was born on 20th September 1902 they had moved to slightly larger accommodation at 12, Grosvenor Cottages. Then, within the next five years they moved to 5, Grosvenor Cottages. Unfortunately, from a family viewpoint, the cottages have been replaced by later buildings (before the year 2000) but the quiet side-road named Whittaker Street still exists. The General Record Office information on birth registrations of Joseph and Jesse's known children is:

1/ 2/ 3	1888	George Joseph	Marylebone	1a 623
10/11/12	1889	Albert	Chelsea	1a 353
4/ 5/ 6	1891	Arthur (Mick)	St. Geo. Han. Sq.	1a 446
10/11/12	1892	Harry	" " " " " "	1a 408
10/11/12	1897	Jessie Mary	" " " " " "	1a 443
10/11/12	1902	Edward William	" " " " " "	1a 426

As noted, 1902 Edward William was to become the writer's father.

From the Bottom of the Pile

Sadly no detail is known of the day to day lives of Joseph and Jessie, but it seems almost certain that they were not isolated in their Pimlico home. It is reasonable to assume that Joseph kept in touch with his brother George in Stanwell. The reason for this is that Joseph's eldest son was called George, and one of George's sons was named Joseph. Brother James was working as a chimney sweep in the Walham Green (now Fulham Broadway) area, and his home was less than three miles from that of Joseph. A grandson of 1814 William was also living in the immediate area, but perhaps as second cousins contact between them had been lost. And finally Jessie's family was near at hand in Marylebone.

We now move forward in time to 1907. On 22nd August 1907 Joseph died in the London Heart Hospital. He was only 45 years age. The cause of death was noted as Morbus Cordis or death of the heart. It was Jessie who registered her husband's death. Then, on 21st September 1907 Jessie died. In her case the cause of death was pneumonia, she was only 39 years of age, and her death was registered by her eldest son George Joseph. Given the family structure noted above, the loss of the breadwinner and his wife within a month would be a tragedy in any age, but in Edwardian England it was even more so because there was no locally based help for Jessie (in the manner of 100 years earlier) after the death of Joseph, and none for the children after Jessie's death. To quote facts, the only known action after the death of widow Jessie was that both Jessie Mary and Edward William were placed in an orphanage.

Having reached this part of the narrative, the writer (1933 Brian Edward, son of 1902 Edward William) asks for the reader's indulgence in moving away from nationally recorded facts to statements that contain elements of early memory and emotion. Joseph died at only 45 years of age. At this point one cannot help but refer back to the comments of Henry Mayhew noted above. It seems probable that Joseph was killed by the nature of his trade. Then, a month later, Jessie died from pneumonia at the age of only 39 years. Why? We now come to a comment made with extreme bitterness and contempt in (the 1950's or 1960's) by 1902 Edward William, the writer's Dad, to both the writer and (on a different occasion) to the writer's younger sister 1937 Brenda Ann. Our Dad stated that his mother Jessie died from drink, and then his father Joseph later died from a broken heart. Clearly Dad had got his facts wrong, and as a five years old child who can blame him, but his opinion of these events both coloured and damaged parts of all his life. Sadly the truth was only discovered after his death in 1970. It is in the record that both 1902 Edward (Dad) and 1897 Jessie (Aunt) were placed in the care of an orphanage after their mother's death. But then what were the opinions of Dad on this? Firstly he remembered that it was at 'about the time of his birthday' that he was committed to an orphanage. He also remembered that his god-parents wanted to adopt him, but were prevented from doing so by the intervention of the church and a 'wicked' female relative (probably an aunt). He had a vague feeling that the god-parents in question were from the chimney sweeping fraternity, and that they were considered 'not good enough'. (Shades of the comments made by Henry Mayhew?) The name of the 'wicked' female relative was not

Joseph, Jessie and their Children

remembered with any accuracy but it was said to be something like Frances or Jessie. Looking now for Dad's aunts on both sides of his family, there is no-one called Frances. There was an 1889 Frances Dowden (G.R.O. 4/5/6 1889 Frances Dowden St. Geo. Han. Sq., 1a 463) in the area at the time, but she was a distant relative of only eighteen years of age at the time, and would she be allowed to exercise influence? There was however a Jessie, namely his own mother. Consider now the social circumstances of 1907. If Jessie wanted an income she would have to work for it. But how could she do this when she had young children? A solution, not uncommon at the time, was that of placing young children in an orphanage during the week, and having the children at home over the weekend. There were variations on that theme, but it seems certain that Edward and sister Jessie were treated in that sort of way after the death of Joseph. Then, on the death of their mother Jessie, the (church) authorities into whose custody the children had been placed would retain them. There is no proof that this is exactly what occurred, but given the social facts in 1907 it seems highly likely. In short, the 'wicked' aunt was probably Dad's mother Jessie who used orphanage facilities for a month, for the best of reasons. With regard to the writer's grandmother Jessie's death there is another social fact of note. Up to the 1920's one of the favourite ways of obtaining an abortion was to get 'dead drunk', usually on 'black and white', namely Guinness and gin. Given the comment of Dad that his mother had drunk herself to death it seems probable that on her youngest son's birthday she became 'dead drunk', collapsed somewhere out in the open, and died the following day from pneumonia. And from the viewpoint of speculation, this unhappy lady may have been trying to obtain an abortion at the time. In any event, grandmother Jessie died on the day after her youngest son's fifth birthday.

Clearly at the time of the death of Joseph and Jessie there were both Dowden and Gorton near-relatives in the area. Never once from either Dad or 1891 Arthur did the writer hear mention of these relatives. It is as if the Pimlico Dowden family were on a desert island. Much later Billy, a son of 1891 Arthur, found the then address of the Seddington family who were the grandchildren of chimney sweep 1859 James. On knocking on the door he announced who he was and asked if he could speak with someone. He had the front door promptly slammed in his face, and no contact was made. From this, and the fact that no other family members were ever mentioned to the writer by Dad or Arthur, it would seem that Joseph was not the family favourite in 1907. But the actual reason for this lack of contact with other family members is unknown.

Now the above, like every essay on earlier generations, was written on the basis of information gained during the 1990's. The notes below were written in the years around 2010 following the publication in 2009 of the 1911 census.

From the Bottom of the Pile

1911 Pimlico

Name	Position	Status	Gender	Age	Work	Born at
George Dowden	Head	Married	M	22	Grocer's Asst.	Paddington
Lily Dowden	Wife	Married	F	20		
Edward Dowden	Son		M	1		

Family living in one room at 98, Lupus Street.

Albert Dowden	Boarder	Single	M	21	Porter	Chelsea
Arthur Dowden	Boarder	Single	M	19	Milkman	Pimlico
Harry Dowden	Boarder	Single	M	18	Baker	Pimlico

All at 53, Ranelegh Grove. (A turning off Lupus Street.)

Jessie Dowden (13 years) and Edward William Dowden (8 years) were both pupils at Hampden House, Broadstairs, Kent at the time of the 1911 census.

The first thing shown by the 1911 census is that the four elder sons of Joseph and Jessie did not retain their family home in Whittaker Street, Pimlico. In 1907 Dad and his elder sister Jessie were placed in an orphanage run by a religious organisation, and we see that they are in the same location as each other in 1911. Now as Dad and Jessie were in the same location in 1911 it seems reasonable to assume that they would have been in the same location since 1907. In later life Dad made many serious charges concerning the cruel treatments to which he and his fellow orphans were subjected in the period 1907 to 1916. One of these was to the effect that he was separated from his sister when, for emotional support, he needed her companionship. Until reading the 1911 census the writer assumed that Dad and Jessie, probably for gender reasons, were placed into separate institutions. It now appears that he was denied access to his sister despite her being on the same premises. Another orphanage cruelty was that boys were required to sleep on their backs with their arms down by their sides. Presumably otherwise they might have fiddled with- - - - need say more? To be found otherwise positioned when in bed merited physical punishment. That the needs of children in care are ignored or frustrated by some of those in authority, or even that cruelty is perpetrated, is clearly not a modern phenomenon. The church (C of E) was never forgiven by Dad for its actions in the orphanage that were inflicted in the name of religious righteousness.

Moving forward from 1911, World War I started on 4th August 1914, and the loudly expressed view at this time was that the war would be over by Christmas. During August 1914 George Joseph (born 1888) enlisted into the army using the names Joseph George (in that order). From the above we can see that he was a married man with a son named Edward who was about three years of age. On attestation on 21-08-1914 George-Joseph stated in writing that he was willing to allot one third of his pay to his wife Lily Harriet Dowden. He was then posted as a rifleman in the King's Royal Rifle Corps (KRRC) on 25-08-1914. The army records do not show that at this time George-Joseph's wife Lily was in the later stages of pregnancy with their second child.

Joseph, Jessie and their Children

On 04-09-1914 George's wife died at the City of Westminster Infirmary. Her cause of death is noted as 1: Pregnancy, and 2: Puerperal Septicoemia. The Sub- district for this record was Chelsea North, but the record did not state as to whether the baby had been born alive. There is then a later letter to George, dated 5th June 1916, from the Children's Aid Committee of 9, South Moulton Street, London W. This is to the effect that 'we are the guardians of his (i.e. George-Joseph's or Joseph-George's) two children' and we are anxious to write to him about their welfare. This letter implies that the child born to George's wife on 04-09-1914 survived despite the death of his/her mother.

Sadly, during an air raid on London during the 1939-45 war the building containing the records for the 1914-1918 war suffered bomb damage. Many of these records survived the immediate effect of the bomb blast, but were then damaged by the water used by the Fire Service in order to save the majority of the building and, in part, its records. The following notes reflect this damage.

Returning now to Joseph's (name used by the army) military activities, he was awarded 7 days (can't determine actual punishment) on 21-12-1914. He was absent (without leave) for fifteen days from 31-12-1914 to 14-01-1915. On 19-01-1915 he was fined 15 day's pay. On 20-01-1915 an inventory of Joseph's missing kit was carried out. On 24-01-1915 Joseph was declared a deserter, and he was struck off the strength of his unit on 16-02-1915. He rejoined from desertion on 02-03-1915. He was awarded 28 days "illegible record" No. 2 on 06-03-1915. Joseph-Georges active service record indicates his embarkation to France on 19-05-1915.

The Battle of the Somme began on 1st July 1916, however there were skirmishes between the opposing sides before that date. In practice Joseph-George was wounded in one of these events on 25th June 1916. He died from his wounds on 18th July 1916 and his body is interred in the WW1 cemetery at Aubigny France.. Clearly widower George left two children as orphans.

With reference to George's children there is a letter from the Children's Aid Committee that appears to be dated between 5th June 1916 and 20th October 1916. This is connected with errors concerning the forwarding of information relating to the children of George. Then on 20th October, there was a further letter from the Committee (to whom?) trying to sort out the muddle. On this the writer has no further information. However a paper from the War Office dated 11th April 1920 states that "the medals awarded to Joseph" should be despatched by registered mail to (The following is noted as recorded, but impossible to translate into simple English): registered mail to guardiMiss M. Douglasan mrs. Elixabeth Butler at 22, East (almost impossible to read but, Stratton Hants?) in trust for the deceased soldier's (blank space) Edward Dowden. There is also a letter from the War Office dated 23rd November (1916?) to Miss M. Douglas, Hon. Sec. Children's Aid Committee, 50, Moulton St. etc. to the effect that articles of personal property (presumably of George) should be despatched to 50, Moulton Street. A form dated 29-11-1917 to Miss M. Douglas etc. asked for the acknowledgement of receipt of 1 watch, 1 disce??, 2 photos, 1 photo case, and birth certificate of George Joseph Dowden.

FROM THE BOTTOM OF THE PILE

(Such are the articles left by George to his son Edward.) In a paper dated 23-02-1921 the latest address of the next of kin is given as 22, East Stratton, Micheldever, Hants. There are technical army-based details concerning the death of George, and these are as follows: 27-06-1916 wounded. 01-07-1916 (from whom received) 30 CSS, ADM. GSW. Mult. 02-07-1916, 42 F.A. Admin. 19-07-1916, 30 CSS, died of wounds. Final document: It appears to read - 25-06-1916 wounded, then 18-07-1916, died of wounds. George's son named Edward J-, presumably J for Joseph. Perhaps in anticipation of the next chapter, the writer has a memory of his father's feelings in relation to his eldest brother George. It was not only one of affection, it was one of a close belonging. Indeed it would seem that George named his son Edward after the writer's father. Similarly the writer's brother Rodney, born in 1943, was, without doubt, named after his Uncle George. In the section Ancestral Documents is noted a copy of a letter from George to the writer's father. It says nothing of substance as was the rule for those in the army in France during the 1914-18 war, but this letter was important as a family momento to the writer's father. George's younger brother, 1889 Albert also joined the army during the 1914-18 war. In Albert's case he was perhaps fortunate in that he was posted by the army to Egypt and survived the conflict. Albert did not get married after his return home, and all that is known is of Albert is that some time after his return to the UK he obtained a job in the despatch department of Harrods in London. In 1930 he had the misfortune to be behind a lorry when its driver placed it into reverse gear and released the clutch. Albert was crushed between the lorry and a wall, and he died of his injuries. He was 40 years of age. Joseph and Jessie's third son, 1891 Arthur, was also in the army during the 1914-18 war. Arthur survived, and because of personal memories of him with my father, aspects of his 1914-18 narrative will be covered in the next essay. 1892 Harry was the fourth and final son of Joseph and Jessie to become embroiled in the 1914-18 war. Harry married a Gertrude Emily Johnson at the Registrars Office, Chelsea on 06-04-1915, and their daughter Jessie Mary was born in Marylebone on 19-05-1915. Harry then joined the army on 09-12-1915. In 1917 Harry's rank was Sapper, and he was attached to Q company of the Royal Engineers in the BEF or British Expeditionary Force on the Western Front in France and Belgium. While on active service Harry was wounded by gas on 05-09-1917. The record then indicates that his condition was described as "Gas Shell poisoning 1027", and as a consequence of this Harry received hospital treatment. It would seem that there was a measure of recovery in Harry's 'post-gas' condition because on 24-01-1918, while on 'Active Service', Harry overstayed his sick leave furlough from Tattoo until reporting at 8:50 pm on 26-01-1918. He was absent for 1 day 23 hours and 20 minutes. His punishment was to be admonished and to forfeit two days pay. Harry was then admitted to hospital again from 15-04-1918 until discharge on 10-06-1918 due to pneumonia. How Harry survived for the next few months is not known, but suffice it to record that he died in the Fort Pitt Military Hospital in Chatham Kent on 28th October 1918 due to pneumonia following influenza. Clearly Harry's lungs were damaged beyond repair by mustard gas or chlorine. He was buried in the cemetery at East Sheen London. During Harry's service the record indicates that his wife Gertrude lived at 27, Little Orford Street, Chelsea, and during this time she received a financial allowance. The details are difficult to interpret, but seem to be noted as follows:

separation allowance 22/-, allotment of pay 7/-, London (??) 3/6: date to which allowances to be paid - continuing. Then, in a paper dated 17-02-1919, Harry's widow Gertrude notes her address as being at 9, Wood Street, Chelsea. On 10-04-1919 Gertrude received a letter from the Ministry of Pensions stating that she has been awarded a pension of 20s 5d a week for herself and one child with effect from 05-05-1919. No more is known by the writer of the fate of Gertrude or her daughter Jessie.   There are only four matters on which the writer is aware concerning the life of 1897 Jessie. She was married, emigrated to or spent some time in Canada before returning to the UK, had a blazing argument with the writer's father (Edward) such that he refused to speak to her again. The reason for this conflict is not known, and to the writer, long after the demise of the parties concerned, the reason is not important. However it is worth noting that the writer's Uncle Arthur maintained a good relationship with both his sister Jessie and his youngest brother Edward. Clearly, from the viewpoint of Arthur, neither of his younger siblings had done something 'beyond the pale'.

Perhaps of all the family narratives this is the saddest. Joseph lost his mother when he was only two years of age, and this must have been very hard on the child. Joseph marries Jessie and they have twenty years of married life together, but then Joseph dies when only 45 years of age. The indications then are that Jessie committed accidental suicide a month later, possibly in order to induce an abortion. Two of Joseph and Jessie's sons are killed in the 1914-18 war and Dowden contact is lost with their widows and children after the deaths of their husbands. Why is it that the writer's father and his elder brother Arthur appeared to know nothing of the fate of their sisters-in-law and their children? In the writer's lifetime he had three cousins whose father's had been killed in the 1914-18 war and who, as a consequence, knew nothing about their paternal family. This type of tragedy is seldom mentioned in histories of this war. In practice my father was mentally damaged beyond repair by the orphanage in which he was placed after losing his mother on the day after his fifth birthday, and was then 'cast adrift' on his fourteenth birthday during the middle of a conflict in which his brother George had just been killed.

There must be easier tales to tell.

And so to Dad, Mum and family.

From the Bottom of the Pile

Dad, with Mum and Family

With the exception of a small part of the preceding essay, the family history thus far is concerned with the lives of people not known personally to either the writer or his immediate forebears. The earlier history essays therefore rely solely on written records from the long distant past. This essay is fundamentally different. There are no written records for the vast majority of the events described. The essay therefore relies upon the memory of the writer in terms of both his own experiences and also the descriptions of events passed to him by others. The intention of the writer, from now referred to as Brian, is to be objective in terms of both the 'facts' described and also the circumstances relating to these 'facts'. Perhaps the reader is to be the judge on the success or otherwise of the writer in this regard.

As noted in the preceding essay, 1902 Edward William, from now referred to as Dad by writer Brian, his elder son, was orphaned on the day after his fifth birthday in 1907. He remained in the care of the orphanage authorities until his fourteenth birthday when, as he told the writer personally, he was discharged to look after himself in the wide world. As an aid in this regard he was given a cleaning job and accommodation in one room, on which he was to feed and clothe himself and pay his rent etc. The year was 1916, World War I was in progress, and the brother with whom he had a special relationship had just been killed in France. Two items of physical and mental brutality suffered by Dad while an orphan are mentioned in the 'Joseph' essay, and are not repeated here, but after Dad's death in 1970 Mum spoke on a number of matters she had previously kept to herself. One of these was that on occasions, in their earlier days together, Dad would talk to her about his orphanage experiences, and as a grown man he then had tears in his eyes and was near to outright crying. Clearly it was a badly damaged youth who was left to fend for himself in 1916. The organisation running Dad's orphanage is not known, but from his remarks to the writer it was religiously based. Dad never forgave 'the church' for the treatment he had received as a child.

No day-to-day details are known of Dad's personal life from the time of his 'launch' into the adult world in 1916 until he met my mother in the mid-to-late 1920's. However from the writers early life there is a distant memory to the effect that Dad spent this period in the area of Pimlico, and this 'feeling' was later strengthened. In November 1953 I (Brian) had a 48 hours pass from my R.A.F. station, and on return home I invited Dad to join me in London to see the Crazy Gang Show at the Victoria Palace Theatre. We arrived at Victoria Station with more than an hour to spare before the start of the show, and I was promptly taken by Dad to a pub (or was it pubs?) for a pre-entertainment drink (or was it drinks?). The point of the tale here however has nothing to do with alcohol. What I suddenly saw was a transformed man. He was immediately at home with, and fully accepted by, the various street-wise members of the 'working' community in that area. Amongst other conversations with people who lived on their wits, he listened to the tales of the local prostitutes and, frankly, he was a man in his element.

From the Bottom of the Pile

I feel sure the reader will understand that finding myself at my father's side, with him being regarded as 'one of the gang' by a coven of local prostitutes, left a permanent impression on me! However I must add that nothing wrong occurred that evening, and I am not suggesting that anything wrong occurred with Dad in his late teens and early twenties. It is simply that it became clear that the back-street London West-End environment was the one in which my father spent his post-1916 life, and it was one in which he thrived. Then he met Mum in the mid-to-late 1920's, and other attractions were encountered.

In continuing to set the scene on Dad's early life I now turn to tales from Dad, of his elder brother Arthur, and Arthur's wife Mabel. These tales were told in the 1950's and early 1960's, however before the telling I must make one point. 1891 Arthur, elder brother of Dad, was known to everyone as Mick. Why is noted in the paragraph below, but suffice it to state now that during the times we were together, he was known to me as Uncle Mick, and Mick is the name I will use in this narrative. By 1925 both Dad and his elder brothers Albert and Mick were working at the Despatch Department of the Harrods Store in Knightsbridge. Dad was a delivery van driver taking orders to, mainly, the high society and diplomatic residences in Belgravia. Like other men at this period he worked all day Monday to Friday and then until lunch-time on Saturday, at which time he received in cash his week's wages. Now any reasonable man can see that such work will generate a thirst, and at this point I recount a tale that was told to me be both my Uncle Mick and his wife Aunt Mabel during their twilight years. This tale was also confirmed by Dad. 'Firstly, no man worth his salt ever let his wife know what he earned. Wage levels were a man's business, and his wife's duty, if not indeed her pleasure, was to manage all family activity on the allowance, generously made, by her husband. Then, if you were involved in arduous work such as that of a despatch department, your first port of call after receiving your wages would be to a local pub to slake the thirst that had developed to an unreasonable level since your last visit. Then, to clear the throat in order to help the beer down, a packet of cigarettes would be purchased and smoked at twice the normal rate. In the local pub one would meet the bookies runner and make one's charitable contribution to the book-makers benevolent fund, the sum in question depending on the results of last week's bets and whether they were made with borrowed money'. I should add that 'off-course' betting was illegal in the UK until about 1960, but that fact was irrelevant to the life of a working man. (I was told that many of Dad's selections 'died in the first furlong', I suspect that most of the others are still running.) Of course these goings-on were well known to the wives who 'unreasonably' (this is Mick's tale) felt that they had a right to some of their husband's money, and here we meet an early version of the battle of the sexes. Aunt Mabel, as told to me personally, left home before lunchtime on Saturday's and, usually pushing a pram containing a young child, walked from Battersea on the south side of the River Thames to the pubs north of the river that were usually frequented after pay-time by her husband Mick and his cronies such as my father. Her intention was to find Mick while he still had her housekeeping money in his pocket. However Mabel, and others in her situation, were up against the cunning of men determined not to lose the just rewards of their labours. In each of the pubs frequented by Uncle Mick, my father and others kept a lookout down the road, and when Mabel was seen approaching, Mick would be

Dad, with Mum and Family

warned. This gave Mick, and similarly his friends, time to take his beer through the serving area and into another bar where it would be rapidly consumed. As Mabel entered the Public Bar, so Mick would leave by (say) the Saloon Bar door, and perhaps to another drinking hole. Once in the Public Bar, Mabel asked if anyone had seen Mick and was either told "No" or was directed to another pub where Mick was known not to be. But yet, despite the above tale, the pub was the centre of entertainment for both husband and wife, and hence on a Saturday evening they went to a pub together. Now the above events have been told with a certain amount of humour and perhaps the reader will feel that it must be an exaggerated parody of the truth. I can only state that the above tale is exactly that told to me by both my aunt and uncle while they were sitting together round their kitchen table. Further to this, Dad verified the story and indicated his involvement in all the above activities.

(The above tale was told to me in Mick and Mabel's home at 2, Darien Road, Battersea. The house was Victorian built (long since demolished), had an outside toilet and no bathroom. At the time both Aunt Mabel and Uncle Mick were in their late sixties and Aunt Mabel had few, if any, teeth. She had the dramatic habit of being able to smile and move her head in a way such that as her head nodded up and down her chin appeared to remain stationary. It was a sight to behold. During the 1914-18 War Uncle Mick spent part of his time as a despatch rider on the Western Front. He also told me that for some time he was a gunner in the Royal Flying Corps. Now in neither of these roles did one have an expectation of life exceeding about 14 days, yet Uncle Mick survived the conflict. I understand that the name Mick came about because he was considered as having "The luck of the Irish".)

Perhaps I should also mention another tale told to me by my father and verified by Uncle Mick. This time it concerns the way in which the authorities in London encouraged those living close to the River Thames into healthy exercise. In order to reduce the earlier incidence of drunkenness, Parliament limited the period of evening opening of public houses to five hours. The authorities on the London County Council then decreed that opening times south of the river would be 5-00 pm to 10-00 pm and north of the river would be from 6-00 pm to 11-00 pm. This gave the working man nearly six hours of drinking time, with a healthy walk in mid-evening across the River Thames for which he was truly grateful. Incidentally, both Dad and Uncle Mick knew, to the minute, how quickly one could cross the river by its various bridges in order to maximise their time of drinking pleasure. Perhaps it is of no surprise that Oscar Wilde wrote that "Work is the curse of the drinking classes". And, given all the above, I ask the reader to ponder on the cultural background of the man who was to meet my mother in the later 1920's, and who was to become her husband and my father.

The above tales were written down in the mid-1990's, and by the standards of the late 20th century they describe a sorry state of affairs. However in the mid-1920's there was no entertainment as it is known today. The pub was the centre of social activity. (Mind you, I didn't think this way when, after a drunken sing-song in a Balham pub one Saturday night, my Uncle Mick tripped down two steep steps and landed on top of me in a heavy heap. He welcomed the soft landing, I had other thoughts!) But despite the above, and at the end of the day, the Mick-Mabel marriage worked, and I believe they were loving partners to the end of their days. And as for Dad, he was a fully paid up member of the gang of cronies that acted as above.

While Dad was enduring his childhood and his later 'good life', Mum, who was born on 16th December 1905, was growing up in the border area of West Kensington and Fulham. Her home was built in the 1850's and was a two-storey four-roomed terraced cottage of about 4m by 5m in ground area. It had an outside flush toilet, a wash-house that was shared with the house next door, and a small back yard with a cinders surface made from the fires of earlier generations. The toilet had a fixed wooden seat I made wet when standing to relieve my bladder, and wash-house water heating was done using a coal fire. The kitchen had a deep sink and one cold tap, bathing was done in a tin bath in the kitchen or in front of the fire in the living room. In my time there was electric lighting and an early electric cooker, but gas fittings were still in place for lighting. Mum did not leave home until shortly before her marriage to Dad in 1933 which meant that until she was 26 years of age she shared her bedroom with her two younger brothers, an arrangement not uncommon at the time.

After discharge from the army in 1918 Mum's father became a tram conductor and hence his family lived on low wages. Despite this he purchased a piano, Mum learned how to read music, and she became a tolerably competent player of this instrument. In short, despite her mean surroundings, her parents tried to give her the best start they could in life. Mum was a bright child at school and left with an above-average report at the age of 14 years. In her youth she was also a conscientious member of her local St. Cuthbert's C. of E. Church. Throughout Mum's life she remained a committed and, when possible, church-going Christian, and in this context one may wonder why she and Dad became married. On leaving school in December 1919 Mum obtained a position 'in service' in a household in King's Road Chelsea. After two years she returned home and obtained a job at the cash-point of the then Timothy Davis store in North End Road Fulham. Now this was a position of trust, especially for a young lady at only 16 years of age, and I recall both Mum and her mother talking with pride about Mum achieving this post. After working for some time at the Davis store Mum obtained the position of a cashier in a company named Slaters, who owned a chain of tea shops in the London area. After working for several years at various branches of Slaters, her final post with the company was at its prestigious and busy store in The Strand. Mum then obtained a post as a cashier at the Harrods store in Knightsbridge, and at this point it must be emphasised that such a post at London's top retailer was very difficult to obtain. In short, she was at the top of the tree in terms of trust in handling other peoples money. In summary Mum had come from mean surroundings, but showed quite clearly that she had the intelligence, desire, spirit and the determination to improve her situation.

On looking at photos of Mum in the late 1920's it is clear that she was a very attractive young lady, and this, in its turn meant that there was no shortage of young men who wished to spend an evening in her company. But, in her own words, Mum was ashamed of her home environment.

Dad, with Mum and Family

She had climbed a certain distance up the status greasy pole and was seen as a skilled worker doing well for herself, yet she lived in a road containing houses fit only for those at the lower end of the social scale. The result was that, without exception until a certain time, every boy-friend who walked her home was led to Archel Road, this being the road parallel to Fane Street in which her own home was located. Mum spoke of the embarrassment of saying "goodnight" outside a house in Archel Road, and then not being able to go in, or to walk towards Fane Street until after the boy-friend was out of sight. Then, in about 1927 or 1928, Mum and Dad met in a Harrods company club activity. The location was the Fulham Swimming Pool at Walham Green (now Fulham Broadway). Mum had met a man she (eventually?) felt able to take home.

In several ways the known details of the courtship of Mum and Dad were unusual. Firstly they became 'an item' for over five years before they were married. In the early days of their courtship Dad became a fully integrated member of Mum's family, it was as if he was adopted by his future parents-in-law. On reflection I think it probable that his courting my mother provided him with his first taste of family life in the form most people (until the 1970's) took for granted. Indeed, he always called my grandmother 'Mum', and he meant it. As part of this integration, and before their marriage, Dad joined Mum on family holidays in places such as Margate and Clacton. They were a happy young couple, and why not.

It was during their courtship that an amusing incident (to Mum when she told the tale) occurred. My mother's Aunt Nancy, a relative by marriage, owned two caravans near the Essex coast. She lived in one caravan and used the other for storage. On one summer's morning my future parents, together with my mother's Aunt Annie and her husband Uncle Ted, visited Aunt Nancy and, after a short time the three ladies went into the local town (Clacton) on a shopping expedition. This left my father-to-be and Uncle Ted with nothing to do, in the middle of a field, on a hot cloudless summer's day. Well, as a species, man is nothing if not inquisitive, and hence it was only natural for the two men to enter the second caravan to peruse its contents. And this they did. To their surprise, as I was told, they then discovered in the van several gallons of home made wine. Now as an aside, from the above it can be seen that Dad did not have a dislike of alcohol, but in this regard he was only an amateur when compared to Uncle Ted. Additionally both men felt that they should do their best to see that Aunt Nancy did not damage herself with any of her home-made fluids. In short, purely for the benefit of Aunt Nancy, the fluids should be subjected to a quality control inspection in case there were any detectable impurities or off-flavours. But sadly, being a very hot day, this proved to be thirsty work. Suffice it to say that when the ladies returned in the late afternoon they found both men lying on the grass, fast asleep, and with bloated sun-burned faces. They received no sympathy. To conclude, when I was told the tale, Dad kept silent.

In terms of the 1920's perhaps Mum's family was similar to many others in their attitudes towards alcohol. There was Uncle Ted who had the reputation of one who drank far too much and there was Uncle Tom who was teetotal. Mum's immediate family was in the middle of the spectrum, with the attitude of so much, but no more. Sadly this did not fit with Dad's culture

From the Bottom of the Pile

because, although not an alcoholic, on many occasions once he started to drink he did not stop until he had drunk too much. Coupled with this, it did not take much alcohol to take him 'over the top'. Against this background came tragedy. At about this time Dad had a 'blazing row' with his sister Jessie. She then emigrated to Canada and later returned, but they never spoke to each other again. In 1930, Dad's brother Albert died as a result of being crushed behind a reversing lorry. This a left Dad with only his brother Mick as a known member of his biological family, and Mick's drinking habits are noted above. Now Mum had a strongly held dislike of Uncle Mick and those around him because of his drinking habits and I seem to remember being told that (85% certainty) Mum extracted a promise from Dad that he would cease drinking in the manner of Uncle Mick. This meant in later years that neither Uncle Mick nor any of his children were welcome in my mother's home. The only way that Dad could see his brother and his family was to travel to Battersea to do so. Now Mum frequently met relatives on her side of the family and so, as a son in his teens who rebelled against her attitude towards Dad's relatives, I probably saw Uncle Mick, Aunt Mabel and their children more often than did Dad from about 1947 to 1965.

Tragedy struck Mum's family in 1932 when her father died at only 60 years of age. Because of his army service in the late 19th century and in the 1914-18 war attempts were made to obtain a pension for his widow, my grandmother. These were unsuccessful and hence my Nan and her sons then had a difficult financial time. My grandmother was always poor, and I recall that Mum and Dad were always generous to her.

Returning to my parent's courting days they had one favourite location for day's out together. I refer to Wimbledon Common. Mum and Dad would travel to 'The Green Man' on Putney Heath and then stroll over Wimbledon Common together. I guess that they probably called in at the 'Hand in Hand' off the south side of the Common because this location was well known to Dad. The point here is that I never heard of them courting in places west of the Fulham-Putney area. Not that is, until late in 1970.

Sadly, on 10th September 1970 Dad died, just ten days before his 68th birthday. His death was sudden, and Mum 'stumbled on' the body of her husband the following morning. I received an urgent telephone call and was asked to come to Mum's home immediately. Shortly after arriving at Mum's home I was asked to retrieve certain papers for passing to the undertaker who was to take Dad's body away, and this I did.

But why interrupt a discourse on my parents courting days with an account of my father's death? It is because of the piece of paper mentioned above. After Dad died, Mum went into a form of depression/shock from which she took a long time to recover. During this time Mum felt it necessary to 'confess' to my wife Sheila a host of trivial matters in which she felt she was at fault. It was as if she needed to 'cleanse' herself. There was only one item of note she spoke about, and that tale is so sad. In very early January 1933 Dad took Mum onto Hounslow Heath, and in that location, and on that cold day, I was conceived. Dad was 31 years of age, Mum was

Dad, with Mum and Family

28 years of age, and they had been going out together for five or six years. Now to the piece of paper -- it gave the date of my parents marriage as 25th March 1933. It was on finding the marriage certificate, with my father's body still in the living room, that I learned some of the truth concerning the beginning of my existence. But my finding this aspect truth as I did is not the sad part of my parents story. In my early teens I asked when Mum and Dad were married and was told 3rd January. Then for years afterwards on that date some form of recognition of their 'wedding anniversary' was made. For example, on one occasion they were given the tickets for a visit to a theatre. Mum and Dad accepted these gifts with (in hindsight) a certain degree of embarrassment, and they never told their children the truth about the date of their marriage. And that is what is so sad, they accepted living most of their lives together with an untruth which to Mum was very uncomfortable, and completely unnecessary.

Returning to the courting days of Mum and Dad, I know from conversations with Dad that he felt he had relatives living in the southwest London area, however he did not know the details. Knowing now what I do, it seems inconceivable that from Uncle Mick he would not have been aware that Harmondsworth was a village that had some form of family relevance. Bearing in mind the damage caused in Dad's early life, is this the reason for the intimacy between Mum and Dad during their visit to Hounslow Heath in early January 1933? We will never know.

As noted, Mum and Dad were married on 25th March 1933. After their marriage they lived in furnished accommodation in the Pimlico area and then moved to a three-roomed 6th floor flat just off Ebury Bridge Road. The address was 151, Wellington Buildings, and it was located less than 0.5 mile from my father's childhood home in Whittaker Street. This flat was my first home.

During the 1920's and 1930's there was a building boom on the outskirts of London which matched that of inner London in the 19th century. In the private sector the properties for sale mainly took the form of 3-bedroomed terrace or semi-detached houses with small front and back gardens. In the public sector the properties for rent included houses with front and back gardens and two or three storey flats. This meant that families with children and people such as elderly couples were catered for. In general terms the private houses were purchased by those who earned their living by clerical or skilled manual means, the public sector housing was rented by those engaged in some form of manual labour. For all, public transport was cheap and frequent enough for travel to the centre of London for work to be an economic proposition. With Mum and Dad living on the sixth floor of a Victorian block of flats, matters such as dragging a pram of the age up and down six floors on a daily basis was a burden, and Mum and Dad intended to increase the size of their family. The result was that they moved into a London County Council (LCC) built rented, terraced, two-bedroomed house on the St. Helier Estate at 20, Winchcombe Road, Carshalton, in late 1936 or early 1937. On 1st May 1937 my sister Brenda was born. On a personal note I do not remember the birth of Brenda, but I do remember visiting Mum in a local rest-home during the ten days period after Brenda's birth. What I remember clearly is the arrival at this time, in a wicker basket, of a tabby kitten named Tinker. Clearly at the time the cat was more important to me than my sister!

From the Bottom of the Pile

It was at about the time of Brenda's birth that Dad obtained his first radio set. It was a Ferguson 7-valves superhet(erodyne) 3-band receiver which meant it could receive short, medium and long wave broadcasts. For its day it was 'top of the range'. The set was placed in the 'front room' of our home, which meant it had pride of place because this room was only used on high days and holidays. Earthing was arranged via a wire from the radio that was soldered to a zinc or zinc coated plate that was buried some two feet below ground level in the front garden. This of course entailed the use of a hole drilled through the front window frame. The aerial socket was connected to a wire that was fed through the house and through one of the upstairs window frames. A pole was then erected at the bottom of the garden which was as high as the eaves of the house and to this pole there was connected (presumably before erection!) a wire long enough to reach back to the house. With the pole wire and the house wire connected, Dad now had his radio receiver, and could tune in to more stations than could most others at the time. Dad then arranged for a loudspeaker connection in the kitchen and thus we had radio in both rooms downstairs. Dad was proud of both his radio and of the manner of its connections.

In about 1938 some goods 'fell off the back' of Dad's delivery van, and he was dismissed with immediate effect from his job with Harrods. The later family view was that 'he had it coming to him', but clearly at the time I had no understanding of what was taking place. Dad then obtained a series of local delivery jobs. The first was delivering bread by horse and cart for Dendy Napper, a Sutton-based baker, then pushing a hand-cart delivering milk for Hill's, a company then based at Rose Hill. This was followed by his final delivery job as a milkman with a horse and cart working for the South Suburban Co-operative Society (SSCS) depot based in William Street, Carshalton. During Dad's employment with SSCS Mum felt obliged to become an SSCS member and shop at the SSCS store at Rose Hill. This she resented because in her view the value of the Co-op dividend was less than the additional cost of buying goods at the SSCS store. Mum had been a cashier, I suspect she was right. It was probably during Dad's employment with Hill's that the 1939-45 war was declared. Dad endeavoured to volunteer for the army but was rejected because he was medically 'grade C', (i.e. his level of fitness was inadequate). He appealed to Dr. Wilmshurst our family doctor, was re-examined, and confirmed as unfit for military service. He therefore spent the war years as a civilian.

Shortly before the 1939-45 war the government of the day offered to families a form of air raid shelter known as the Anderson shelter. This comprised a series of corrugated iron sheets shaped such that they could be bolted together to form a two metres long inverted U shape. This shape was then dropped about 80 cm into a purpose built hole in the ground. and a corrugated back and front fitted. The front had a small entrance at ground level. In our own case the inside of the shelter had a concrete floor and sides which were some 12 cm thick and 80 cm high. Resting on the sides were two bunks each about 1.8 m long and 80 cm wide and on both the floor and the bunks were placed bedding material. The outside of the shelter was covered with earth which was planted with mint. This was supposed to give good stability to the outside soil. Hopefully the four of us would be safe in the event of bombing by Hitler's Germany. At the time in question the people living next door in number 22 did not want an Anderson shelter,

Dad, with Mum and Family

and they then moved away. The new tenants did want an Anderson shelter, but by then it was too late to acquire one.

In the period 1940-41 there occurred the Battle of Britain and then the 'Blitz'. Both these events involved the sky immediately over our home area and, perhaps, there are several events worthy of record. At that time communities came together and acted for the common good, and hence any decent family would help a neighbour when such was needed. Thus our new neighbours shared our shelter during the worst of the aerial conflict. We were a family of four for which the shelter was designed, next door there was a similar family of four, with the mother also pregnant at the time. We had, shall I say, closely cosy nights in each others company as we shared the shelter together. One night our front door and some windows were blown in by a high explosive bomb that had landed nearby. On that occasion the gas main was damaged, we lost our gas supply, and cooking was done in the oven over a fire in the front room (despite a locally broken gas main). More seriously there was a loss of life and the destruction of houses in the incident. On another night a German bomber released his load of incendiary bombs from nearly overhead. On this occasion the bombs landed in a nearly straight line path in the back gardens in our part, and on our side, of Winchcombe Road. Dad and others left their shelters to smother the flaring magnesium bombs, with one neighbour, afraid to leave his shelter entrance and calling "Look after my chickens". Dad's views were, and still are, not repeatable. There was however an incredible follow-up to the incendiary bomb night. On the next occasion that Mum attempted to light a fire under the copper (for hot water) it would not light and smoke filled the kitchen. Dad opened the door giving access to the chimney and found the remains of a partly burned incendiary bomb. Some months later the same lighting problem occurred again. This time Dad attacked the chimney with a sweepers brush and a second, partially burned incendiary bomb was recovered. With a lateral shift of only 10 cm either of these bombs would have fallen through the roof tiles into the loft space and we would have lost our home. During a later night a rather shaken Dad returned home on his bicycle. A shard of red hot razor-sharp shrapnel some 15 cm long had descended to earth and, just missing Dad, had buried itself into the road surface. This was almost certainly a fragment of shell fired into the night sky from the battery on Mitcham Common. If you were out during an air raid warning, you couldn't even trust your friends not to kill you.

As a milkman Dad was earning a minimum wage and, in my parents eyes, a financial supplement was needed. Thus in 1941 or 1942 Mum obtained a clerical job at the St. Helier Hospital. This job lasted until shortly before the birth of my younger brother Rodney George on 11th March 1943. In this instance the name George was given in memory of Dad's eldest brother George Joseph who was killed during the 1914-18 war. At the time many neighbours suggested to Mum that it was unfortunate, if not indeed irresponsible to have a baby at that time. Mum's proud response was to the effect that, "If that bloke Hitler thinks he's going to upset my family plans, then he has another think coming." Incidentally I was kicked out of bed in the middle of the night in order that Mum could give birth in my bedroom. Of course I blame Rodney for this!

From the Bottom of the Pile

In 1942 Mum and Dad decided that we would spend the summer holiday period in the hopfields of Kent, and we travelled to Marden to be met, as pre-arranged, by a local farmer. Perhaps this episode was induced by my parents need for money at that time. However picking hops (by hand in those days) is thirsty work and I suspect that evenings spent at the 'local' nullified any gain.

During Dad's time as a milkman I was 'encouraged' to help him with his milk-round before school, over the weekends, and during holiday periods. This meant that on occasions I arrived late at school. In 1943 my class teacher regarded this as an intolerable state of affairs, and Dad was threatened with being reported to the education authorities and hence being prosecuted if he did not change his ways with me. Suffice it to say that he then conformed with the law. In contrast, on another occasion it was Dad who complained to the education authorities. During the war there was no production of toys and similar items that could be used by children. Against this background, if at my local school a child lost a ball on (say) the flat roof of a toilet block then the caretaker would retrieve the ball in the evening and give it to his dog. On one occasion I lost a ball in this manner and, wishing for its return, I went back to school in the evening, climbed up a drainpipe, and retrieved my ball. But I was caught by the caretaker who then called the police and accused of being one of a gang who continually caused problems. The result was my being escorted home between two burly policemen. On being informed of the accusations Dad exploded, and in turn advised the police of the caretakers well known conduct. Suffice it to say that the caretaker received a written warning from the education authority, and would have been evicted from his house if he was later dismissed. He kept his job, and presumably must have changed his ways.

In late 1943 or early 1944 Dad left the SSCS and obtained a job as a fitter's mate at the power station in Beddington. This job entailed night work and many an unhappy time occurred when Dad could not sleep during the day due to external noise. Then, in the early summer of 1944, the south east of England was subjected to attack by the V-1 flying bomb or 'doodle bug'. As children we spent most of our time during the day in the school air raid shelters and hence the Government put into operation its prepared evacuation plans. These involved the evacuation to 'safe' areas of schoolchildren and nursing mothers with children under two years of age. As Rodney was under two years of age Mum was evacuated with Rodney, and hence Brenda and I were evacuated with our mother. After leaving home at about 6-00 am on a sunny summer morning, Mum with her three children and all necessary luggage, joined other evacuees at the top of Winchcombe Road. The group then made its way to Carshalton Station where we were met by other evacuees. We were then transported to the main line Victoria Station, by Underground to Euston Square, by foot to main line Euston Station and hence onto a steam hauled 'evacuation train'. During parts of the 'to London' journey we were joined by more evacuees, and at Euston there was a 'train load' of people to be evacuated. I have no memory regarding feeding arrangements on the train, but do not recall being hungry during most of the journey to our final destination. Incredibly, none of the evacuees had any idea regarding our final destination, all one could do was to look at the passing station name plates during the

Dad, with Mum and Family

journey. After some six hours the train stopped at a sequence of destinations and at each of these a group of people disembarked. Our turn came at Shaw, a cotton mill area between Oldham and Rochdale. From the station we were led to a community centre in which we were fed on tea, bread, and a copious quantity of Lancashire Hotpot. After some three hours we were then led to a nearby house for over-night sleep. My memory of that night is of being cramped and cold in a very damp location and Mum did not consider such living conditions acceptable. Mum saw the local people concerned with accommodating evacuees the following day with the result that we were transferred to two neighbouring '1930's' terraced houses. The idea was that Brenda and I would sleep in one house and Mum and Rodney in the other. Meals would be eaten in 'Mum's house'. This arrangement quickly broke down with the result that all four of us lived in Mum's house. I use the term 'Mum's house', but of course it was lived in by a family who considered it fully occupied, and that created difficulties such as insufficient space or crockery for meals to be eaten together. Then there was strict rationing at the time, and how could one separate out the flour or sugar etc. being used by one family as opposed to the other? Both Mum and the family on whom we were imposed had a very difficult time, and it is much to the credit of all concerned that matters proceeded as well as they did. On one or two occasions we were visited by Dad, and apart from a 'clogs' episode (part of my story) these visits went well. By September the flying bomb menace had diminished and we returned home. There was at that time a V-2 rocket menace, but that was regarded as being both short-term and acceptable. There were some difficulties on the return home due to Dad having taken advantage of our absence to effect a clear out of unwanted artifacts. The problem was that goods unwanted by Dad were often wanted by others in his family, and this created problems.

Life at home continued normally until the end of the war in 1945, but two tales are probably worth the telling. During the war, and also afterwards, there was severe rationing of meat products and items such as eggs. Thus Dad, and also most neighbours constructed rabbit hutches, chicken runs, and even in Dad's case a small puddle of water in which he hoped some ducks would feel at home. These creatures do of course attract rats, and our cat Tinker proved to be a superb rat catcher. We knew this because rats surplus to his food requirements were presented to us on the back door step. But Tinker also had a taste for gourmet food, and on the occasion that Dad bought some ducklings, he saw two of these disappear down Tinker's throat in next to no time. Dad ran down the garden, grabbed Tinker by the scruff of the neck, and proceeded to grate the cat's nose up and down the fine wire mesh on the ducklings home. When he let go of Tinker, the humiliated and hurt cat shot away faster than he had ever been seen to move previously. Tinker stayed away from home for about a week, and after his return he had lost all his taste for duck. Tinker was not the only one who lost his taste for certain types of food. We ate so many rabbits during the war that even in my later life I cannot stand the taste of the little beastie. The chicken tale is somewhat different. She was named Lucy and was a family pet because of her regular production of eggs. But the day came when she ceased laying and Dad felt that the time had come for her to make her final contribution to the welfare of the family. Mum said to Dad if you kill that bird I will cook it, but I will not eat it. He did, she did, and then didn't. I recall a lovely meal. It should be added that at that time, regardless of rationing, any form of poultry was a treat. At the time of writing, chicken is the cheapest of meats.

Dad left the power station with its shift work at about the time of the end of the 1939-45 war, and for the rest of his working life he earned his living working with or maintaining production machinery in a range of locations. One of Dad's later jobs was at the (then) Paynes Poppet factory in Beddington. In this employment he was allowed to eat as many sweets as he wished during working hours, and of course he soon became sick of them. A later post was as a production operative at the Vinyl Products factory in Carshalton, and in this role he was working at the start of the post-war plastics industry. He may have had other employment after his Vinyl Products job, but if any, these are not recalled. Suffice it to say that I have no recollection of Dad being out of work. Dad's final job, which he had for a period of about five years, was as a maintenance mechanic working on the steam plant then used to provide hot water and driving forces for the laundry in the then Mental Hospital at Banstead.

In 1945 Mum and Dad booked our first family holiday. The idea was that a hut in Gurnard Bay on the Isle of Wight would be rented for four weeks and that Mum, Rodney, Brenda and I would spend four weeks on the island, with Dad and Grandma being on the island for part of the time. Unfortunately Rodney caught impetigo just before the holiday period and was quarantined at home. In the end, Dad and I spent just one week on the island. The week was one of pleasure and pain. Pleasure because each morning we would pick large quantities of mushrooms and have a huge breakfast of fried mushrooms and scrambled egg made from dried egg powder. Pain by standing outside a local pub every evening while Dad enjoyed himself at the bar. (At that time entrance to a pub was forbidden to those under 16 years of age.)

Also in 1945 I passed the scholarship to Sutton County Grammar School. The school was a middle-class institution that took paying pupils until 1944-5, and hence I was removed from my working class scholastic background. Sadly Mum and Dad showed that they had no understanding of my new situation. They visited the school for the one and only occasion before the start of my first autumn term and negotiated that I should be excused the requirement to wear school uniform on the grounds of cost and rationing restrictions. I thus attended my new school wearing a blue jacket while every other boy wore a red one. Then in 1948 an incident occurred when I desperately needed parental support. I didn't get it, and my future school life was blighted as a consequence. Frankly, for me, both Mum and Dad were out of their depth as far as the Grammar School system was concerned. They may, though I suspect not, have improved as their other children also passed the scholarship for entrance to a local grammar school.

In the later months of 1946 Mum became pregnant again, and for the second time I was kicked out of bed, now for the birth of my sister Pauline Margaret in May 1947. Normal practice of the time would have dictated that Pauline's second name was one of Mum's, but the name Alice was disliked and the name Colchester was positively loathed. Pauline's second name is thus Margaret because that was a name that Mum liked. Now with four children, for Mum and Dad, our house was too small and we moved about 1 km to 28, Whitby Road. The new house was end of terrace, giving space on the side for items such as a bicycle, had two bedrooms as before, but had a small front room that could be used as a third bedroom.

Tinker the cat was the loser in the move. He was kept in the new home for several days, had things such as butter put on his paws, but insisted on returning to his previous haunts. But the war was over, rabbits etc. were no longer kept, the vermin of previous years was no longer in the area, and Mum and Dad's previous neighbours were not willing to leave any food out for Tinker's benefit. (They were not asked to provide Tinker with a home.) With a heavy heart, and resentment towards their previous neighbours, Dad ended the unhappy saga by having Tinker 'put to sleep'.

In 1948 Brenda passed the scholarship examination and was offered a place at Wallington Grammar School for Girls. Mum and Dad were proud of the fact that their two elder children had both passed the scholarship examination, but the expense of this put a strain on the household budget. I do not recall Brenda having any 'uniform' difficulties.

Unfortunately Dad was a heavy smoker and as a result, in the early 1950's, he developed a growth on his lungs. The growth had to be surgically removed if Dad was to live, but at the time such an operation was a very serious matter. Dad went into St. Helier Hospital and part of his lung was removed. Picture now the scene the following day. Dad is in a side room and he lights a cigar in celebration of finding himself still alive. The surgeon and his entourage then enter Dad's room. "Put that out" instructs the ward sister in an officious voice, "Carry on smoking" said the surgeon, "After what Mr. Dowden has been through he deserves a good smoke". Dad was very proud of that moment. It was then several weeks before Dad was fit to return to work.

Sadly the Tinker tale above is not the only 'difficult' cat story. After Tinker, Mum and Dad had a black cat with traces of white called Nigger. Like Tinker, Nigger also had an interest in pursuing the local vermin population, but he did not possess Tinker's level of skill. On several occasions Nigger was bitten in the neck, and these wounds turned into nasty abscesses, Mum or Dad then took Nigger to the vet for treatment. Then one evening Dad confided to me that he just could not continue paying the vet's bills generated by Nigger, but then also Mum would not contemplate Dad taking Nigger to the vet for his 'final' journey. Dad then stated that somehow he would have to commit 'cat murder', but had no idea how to do this without arousing Mum's suspicions. The time in question was about November 1951, I had left school and in my place of work I had access to chloroform. The solution was simple. I would bring some chloroform home, and Dad could put Nigger to sleep. Come the evening in question Dad, who had despatched more rabbits, chickens and so on that I care to think about, could not bring himself to despatch poor Nigger. So with Dad's help Nigger was coaxed onto my lap and I placed a pad soaked with chloroform close to, and then against, Niggers nose until he stopped breathing. The cat quickly fell asleep and I feel certain that it was a painless time for the cat, but not for Dad. While the cat was on my lap Dad repeated a mantra to the effect that if the cat lived he would spend all his money on necessary vets bills. But the cat did not live, and its body was placed outside the house in a sleeping position under a lean-to. Dad left for work the following morning and when Mum woke me she said that poor Nigger had died in the night in the lean-to. Why Dad never 'saw' the cat while collecting his bike on his way to work was never questioned -- at least by Mum. And to her dying day Mum never knew the truth about Nigger.

Mum's two brothers were married in 1944 and 1948, leaving my grandmother, Nan, living alone during her twilight years in 15, Fane Street Fulham. But Nan was suffering from breast cancer and in 1949/1950 she was no longer able to support herself. She then moved into Mum and Dad's home, sleeping in the small front room that had been Brenda's bedroom. And that was the natural thing to do in those days, because children looked after their older generation. After some six months, on a warm summer's day, Nan died at 69 years of age. Now Nan had left a Will that she made after the death of her husband in 1932, and this Will was dated 1933. Clearly money values had changed between 1933 and 1950. In her Will Nan left a property in Dawes Road, Fulham valued at £300, and the arrangement was that each of her two sons should have £100 and that Mum should have the remainder. In the period 1933 to 1950 property values had risen, but the property had badly deteriorated, with result that its 1950 value was £1,000. Mum gave each of her brothers £300, paid the various costs of Nan's demise, and had less than £300 left for herself. In this matter I feel that Mum and Dad deserve full marks for integrity.

In 1955 Rodney was the third of the Dowden children to pass the scholarship examination. Rodney, like myself ten years earlier, accepted the offer of a place at Sutton County Grammar School. In 1958 Pauline followed the example of her elder siblings and was offered a place at the Wallington County Grammar School for Girls. To the best of my knowledge the Dowden family was the only one on the St. Helier Estate to have (all) four children attain a grammar school education. Mum and Dad were both proud of this achievement.

By the time of her mid-teenage years Brenda had grown into a very attractive young lady, and of course the local young men behaved accordingly. In this period she began a relationship with a young man some 2.5 years older than herself called Brian Hyatt, and, as happens in life, this relationship ended. However Brenda's Brian and I had a common interest and continued to see each other, and hence Brian H. continued to meet Brenda if we went together to my home. There is a tale worth the telling now from my generation's point of view, but I won't do so here because this is a narrative concerning my parents. Suffice it to state therefore that Brenda became pregnant, and Brian H was the father of the baby to be. Brenda was 19 years of age. From this point on Brian H became persona non grata as far as all members of the Dowden household were concerned, and the question for Mum and Dad was how should they handle the situation. Firstly Mum and Dad wished to support their daughter in whatever way was possible. Secondly, at the time, there was a terrible social stigma attached to the production of children outside wedlock, and this made it impossible for Brenda to remain at home during her pregnancy. Mum, Dad, and Brenda were on the horns of a dilemma. But, as recorded earlier in this narrative, Mum was a highly religious lady who regularly attended the local

Dad, with Mum and Family

C. of E. church, and hence Mum took advice from her church priest. The result was that Brenda was accommodated at Addiscombe in a church-run home for girls (who had morally strayed!) for most of her period of pregnancy. Sadly it was as if the church authorities were carrying on where they had left off with Dad. Living conditions were very poor and the girls were made to understand that they were "fallen women" now in receipt of charity. Church attendance was strongly encouraged if not indeed enforced. The one incident concerning living conditions that comes to mind is that the very large loaf of bread used as part of the Harvest Festival celebration was being fed to the girls for more than two weeks after being baked. Mum and Dad both knew of Brenda's distress, Mum seemed to me to feel that anything done by the church must be for the best, Dad was simply paralysed. As the time came for the birth of Brenda's baby she was transferred to a church-run delivery home in Kingston. The family was relieved that Brenda had left Addiscombe, but did not realise what was to come. The treatment meted out to the girls in the Kingston home was so bad that at a later date those responsible for the home's day-to-day operation were charged with, and then imprisoned for, cruelty. For neither location were Mum or Dad mentally equipped to take the relevant authorities to task for their treatment of Brenda, and this is sad. But then they did their best to support their daughter in the only way that appeared to be open to them.

After Brenda's daughter Julie was born, both mother and baby returned home for a short period of time, but the narrative must now digress onto the social conditions of the late 1950's. The later situation whereby unmarried mothers were given local authority housing and a host of social security benefits did not exist. The young mother had to support herself and her child, and if child support from the mother or others close to her was not possible, then the child would be forcibly removed from the mother and placed for adoption. Against this background there was no financial support from Brian (he wasn't asked, but we understood that he would have resisted). Neither Mum nor Dad felt able to contemplate the prospect of having both Brenda and Julie at home, and hence arrangements were made (by Mum) for Julie to be fostered by a lady who lived about 0.5 km away. This arrangement enabled Brenda to return home, to earn the cash needed for the support of Julie, and to have regular contact with her daughter. The attitude of mind was that Julie was a fully fledged member of the Dowden family who was on temporary loan due to the circumstances of the time. As if to emphasise this point, on one occasion Julie was lying in her pram inside the hall in Mum and Dad's house in Whitby Road, the front door was open. Then a social worker and a lady, without so much as a 'by your leave' entered the hall. Mum soon 'got wind' of the situation and when she confronted the intruders she discovered that the lady was looking for a baby to adopt. There was no question now of Mum not having the ability to deal with someone in apparent authority. Both people were told, in no uncertain terms, that her grandchild was not, and never would be, available for adoption by anyone. Personally, I recall Mum's anger that evening. In the fulness of time Brenda and Brian H were reconciled, and in October 1959 they were married.

Shortly before the wedding of Brenda and Brian, my girl-friend and future wife Sheila suffered from a nasty kidney condition. Her problem required close medical attention and also bed rest

From the Bottom of the Pile

for about a week, meaning that it was not practicable for Sheila to receive this treatment at her father's home. Mum and Dad were asked if Sheila could be nursed in our home and without hesitation the answer was "yes". But at that time my parents and 12 years old Pauline slept in the front bedroom, Rodney and I slept in the back bedroom, and Brenda slept in the front room downstairs. By mid-20th century standards the house was full. The solution was for Sheila to occupy my bed and sleep in the same room as 16 years old Rodney, an arrangement he accepted (I believe) without complaint. I then slept in Sheila's bed-sit in Tooting with the permission of all concerned at that location. This incident demonstrated a generosity of spirit by Mum and Dad, particularly when we both felt that my parents never fully accepted Sheila for many years.

As the 1950's moved into the 1960's so also Mum and Dad seemed to move into a quieter phase of life. Brenda and her Brian were married, Sheila and I were married in 1960, and in that year both Rodney and Pauline were progressing well in their grammar schools. Uncle Mick no longer caused marital upsets in the manner of earlier years, if only because he had ceased his previous drinking habit and also no longer visited my parent's home. Then, in the earlier part of 1965 I received a message that Uncle Mick had died, and that Aunt Mabel would like to see Dad and I. I took Dad to the flat in which Uncle Mick and Aunt Mabel were living and Dad saw his brother for the last time. As in many instances, this particular evening is worthy of a tale in its own right, but this narrative is about Mum and Dad, and suffice it to say that Dad was very upset in a dignified way about losing his brother. Whether Dad's sister Jessie was alive at the time is not known, she was not mentioned during the evening with Aunt Mabel, and clearly Dad felt that he was the last survivor of his generation.

Sheila and I were married in the Baptist Church in Edenbridge on 23rd July 1960. For us life followed a fairly normal course except that we never felt that Sheila was fully accepted as a member of my family from a 'she's one of us' point of view. Having started our married life with no assets we saved to accrue a deposit for the mortgage on our first home and then obtained a limited amount of furniture. Only then, when our home situation appeared stable, did we think of starting a family, and our first son Christopher was born on 26th May 1964. At this time I was approaching 31 years of age and Sheila and I were of the view that we should have our children as quickly as reasonably possible. Other factors came in to play at this time, but suffice it to state now that our second son Gerald was born on 23rd September 1965. After Gerald's birth (at home), and when Sheila and the baby were settled down I phoned Mum and Dad with the news. There must have been a quiet response because I cannot remember any reaction at the time. However no attempt was made by either Mum or Dad to travel the four miles to see either us or their new grandchild. I telephoned to ask when we could expect a visit and was told by Mum that a letter written by Dad and addressed to me was in the post. No more was said by Mum at the time, and this unexpected response left us with a feeling of foreboding. Within a day or so the letter, addressed to me and marked 'Private and Confidential', arrived. I was at work when the letter was delivered, and although Sheila and I have no secrets from each other we do not open each others mail, thus the letter remained closed until my return home from work at about 10-00 pm. Sheila was thus left looking at an item of 'suspicious' mail for about twelve

Dad, with Mum and Family

hours. On returning home I opened the letter, and in it my father informed me that no son of his would make his wife pregnant again so soon after the birth of his first child. The news was devastating. Sheila was distraught and with more or less immediate effect she was no longer able to breast-feed Gerald. Our son did not therefore receive all the 'early-life' benefits from his mother's milk that are so desirable. Also, with Sheila already in a melancholic state (for reasons given in 'my' narrative) she became clinically depressed and was medically treated accordingly. Within a day or so I called round at my parents home and received a cool reception. Then, despite knowing the name of our son Dad asked, "What are you calling the baby"? "Gerald", I replied. "Huh, piss-pot"' he responded, (a slang name for a commode or chamber-pot was 'jerry'), alluding to the fact that the name Gerald is often shortened to 'Gerry'. My father then repeated the allegation in the letter. In the event I was too upset to challenge my father directly on whether he was disowning me on the grounds of my behaviour, or whether he was accusing Sheila of adultery. But from the ensuing conversation it was made clear that I was not being personally criticised, and hence in their eyes Sheila was an adulterous wife. Moving forward many years, from Gerald's facial features there is no doubt about his parentage.

There was unexpected fall-out from the above incident. Mum and Dad were held in high regard in the family, and when it became known that Sheila and I were in conflict with my parents, curiosity 'as to why' was expressed by family members. I do not know if my parents said anything, but we said nothing in order to prevent the spreading of a conflict. The conclusion by some was therefore that "We must be in the wrong, because of not talking on the matter." This was a hard time. With regard to Sheila and Gerald, Dad acted and Mum kept silent on the matter. Should I keep silent now, knowing that my parents cannot reply to the above? The reader can form an opinion. But the above incident was the most important way in which my parents impacted upon my marriage and my adult life. The events were also a part of their life, and hence are recorded.

Later that year, in December 1965, Rodney married Mary Doyle. Perhaps it was Rodney's impending marriage to Mary that forced a measure of contact between Sheila and I and my parents, because I was the best man at Rodney's wedding. But be that as it may, we began speaking to Mum and Dad again, but matters were never as they were before the Gerald incident. Indeed, for me the close attachment I felt towards my father was permanently broken.

In 1965 sister Pauline became engaged to be married to Robin Davey. As I understand matters Mum and Dad accepted both the situation and Robin into their household. Then in 1966 Robin and Pauline began making arrangements for their wedding and Mum and Dad stated that they would not give permission for the marriage to proceed. Now Pauline and Robin were determined to go ahead with their plans and the position was this: Under the then law any person under 21 years of age required parental permission to marry. Pauline was only 19 years of age. Parental refusal to give consent could be nullified by a magistrate, and this was not uncommon at the time. Also at this time Parliament was debating the issue of bringing the age of majority down to 18 years, and this would affect Pauline's status. Then, at that time both

From the Bottom of the Pile

Pauline and Robin had been together for at least a year, they were both in steady employment and hence could support themselves. In my view no magistrate would deny Pauline and Robin the right to marry each other. I argued with Mum and Dad that the only consequence of their refusing permission for the marriage would be that of alienating both their daughter and their new son-in-law, and that such action would be foolish. They gave way to the argument and Pauline and Robin were married in the summer of 1966. Events some 15 years later make one wonder about the decision of Pauline and Robin, but that is part of Pauline's story.

In keeping with the earlier decision concerning children conceived by Sheila and I, Nigel was born on 29th March 1967. On this occasion there was no stupid letter from my father. Had he learned a lesson from the 'Gerald' episode? The question was never asked.

As noted above Dad retired in September 1967. Then in 1968 or (more probably) 1969 Mum was taken into hospital for a gall bladder operation. She went into hospital as a middle-aged woman, and came out as an old lady. The operation appeared to add ten years to her age, although one must accept that it probably saved her life. During the time Mum was in hospital Sheila often went to Whitby Road to take Dad some food etc., and to see that he was well looked after. It was then, some ten years after he had first met Sheila, that he behaved in a truly affectionate way towards the lady in my life. Indeed, without any form of prompting, he told Sheila that in his previous opinion of her, he was wrong. What a shame that he did not open his eyes at an earlier date. Following his actions at the time of Gerald's birth we were all the losers.

As mentioned above, in the very early hours of 10th September 1970 Dad died. He was ten days short of his 68th birthday. On the evening of 9th September Mum had gone to bed in the normal way, leaving Dad downstairs with a book and a supply of home-made wine. It was now normal procedure for Dad to have a drink and a read before retiring to bed at about 1-00 am. At some time, presumably not long after midnight, Dad undressed himself, put on his pyjama trousers, put one arm in a pyjama jacket sleeve and was putting the other arm in the other sleeve when his heart stopped beating. He collapsed, and I was told that he was dead before his body reached the floor. Mum woke up at about 6-00 am and realised she did not have her husband at her side. She went downstairs and saw the body of her husband on the floor of the lounge. The shock was profound. Via a neighbour I was called to the house and was asked to take charge of procedures such as calling undertakers, finding necessary papers, and so on.

For many years Mum and Dad had a small cupboard unit in their bedroom whose door was locked by means of an over-sized padlock and hasp. In this cupboard was located anything that Dad wished to keep secret, even from Mum. On the morning of Dad's death Mum gave me the key to the padlock and asked me to find her wedding certificate and any other papers of interest. Two items come to mind. Firstly I found the wedding certificate which was wanted by the undertakers. Now in the earlier part of this narrative concerning the latter part of my parents courting days I mention the fact that I was conceived some 2-3 months before Mum and Dad were married. I will not repeat the tale now, however for me, it was on the day of my

Dad, with Mum and Family

Dad's death I found out the truth of my parents earlier actions, and on that same day Mum knew that the truth was now known. Of course, we did not discuss this matter on that occasion. The second item found was a bank book about which Mum had no prior knowledge. The book was retrieved, opened, and it led to the following realisation. When Dad retired he was entitled to a small occupational pension as a result of his service at the Banstead Mental Hospital. However the pension was small and Dad accepted an offer of a lump sum of about £500-00 in place of the pension. (At the time a working man's gross wage was about £100-00 a month.) Mum knew nothing of this arrangement, and within 18 months of Dad's retirement he had spent all the money without there being any form of benefit to his wife or his home. The assumption made was that the cash was donated to the publicans and bookmakers benevolent funds. That Dad behaved as he did can be regarded as being both demeaning and dishonest. One can say, "What a sad end"! But given the impact on Dad of his early life, let he/she who is totally innocent throw the first stone.

After Dad's death Mum went into a state of depression in which she felt it necessary to talk, at least to Sheila and sometimes to me, on a whole host of personal matters on which she felt guilty. These matters were the trivial peccadillos of which we are all guilty, and we properly regard them as being part of life's rich pattern. Not so with Mum, she needed to talk her conscience clear. One sad fact is that after her operation she could not be intimate with Dad, and for that she felt guilty. Then of course the events of my conception were discussed and as Mum spoke she held her hands close to the lower part of her stomach. "I knew immediately that I had a baby in there." she stated. And clearly she was pleased by this 'knowledge'.

After Dad died, Mum's income was such that the rent and rates on her house was paid out of social security funds. But of course she was living alone. Also at this time Robin and Pauline, with their children, were finding their flat unsuitable as accommodation for a growing family. The result was that in the early 1970's Robin, Pauline etc. moved in with Mum. Now this was a serious move because Robin and his family were on the housing list for family accommodation. The point here is that on the St. Helier Estate it was common practice for children to move back to their parent's homes without declaring the move and hence household income. This left the social security fund continuing to pay rent and rates, which was illegal, but many did not care. In Mum's case the move of Robin etc. into her home as lodgers was declared with the result that Robin became responsible for paying rent and rates to the then property owners -- the London Borough of Sutton. Then, in the mid-1970's the borough took ownership of some one bedroomed wardened flats in Sutton and Mum was offered the tenancy of one of these. The offer was accepted and Mum's last home was in this wardened accommodation. Meanwhile, because Robin and Pauline were 'officially' at 28 Whitby Road they were offered the tenancy of the house, which of course they accepted.

The reader may recall that Mum underwent a serious operation in 1969 and appeared to age suddenly as a consequence. By the mid-1970's this meant that Mum was in receipt of a cocktail of drugs in which 'the balance' had to be kept 'just right', and hence her life in the flat was not easy. However Mum did develop a life while in the flat. She became an active member of the congregation of the local (St. Barnabas) church, she was one of a group of 'merry widows' who previously lived in the St. Helier Estate, and she developed a lovely friendship with a man called Sam. We understood at the time that Sam had proposed to Mum but she declined. As Mum said, "I have lost one husband and I do not wish to lose another. And in any case I have always been your Dad's, and that is how I wish to remain." Sam died some four years after the start of their friendship. As Mum progressed into her mid-seventies she became frail and also aware of her own mortality. At this time she would say to me, "Please tell me what you would like when I am gone." My reply was always the same, "Mum I do not wish to discuss the breaking up of your home during your lifetime. After you have gone your four children will meet together and, in our usual friendly manner, we will jointly decide what goes where." It didn't happen that way because others were happy to say to Mum what they would like, but what happened after Mum's death is not part of her story.

In the autumn of 1981, when Mum was 75 years of age, she went to Brenda and Brian's bungalow for a few days. While away from her normal medical supervision Mum's drugs cocktail went out of control, she was taken to a local hospital, and after a few days she died. I think it fair to say that on this occasion she did not wish to recover because she said to Sheila that she now wished to meet her husband again. Also it seems likely that she knew her fate because she spent much of her time in hospital writing 'goodbye' letters to various people.

Mum left a Will with myself (Brian) and a local solicitor as joint executors. In practice Mum left no artifacts with financial value, and indeed her funeral costs exceeded the sum of money in her flat and bank account(s). Mum's funeral, like Dad's 11 years previously, did in practice cost their children money. Of course there was no problem in the children seeing to it that the right thing was done for our mother, but persuading a solicitor that there was no money in the kitty to cover any executor costs proved to be a problem. Finally the solicitor revoked his executor role, much to the relief of the writer.

Mum's funeral was held from her previous home in Whitby Road. Her body was cremated at the Roehampton Crematorium as were the bodies of both Dad and Mum's Mum. Her ashes were scattered in the same area as that of her husband and her mother.

Appendix

Looking back to Elizabethan London it was recorded in 1571 that "Supplye Guydon, a Frenchman and a servant, has been in England for about four years past and is of no church". Further records in the 1590's show that Supplye was paying taxes and then in 1600, and as a married man, he was in receipt of parish relief. Did Supplye have a son named Toucher who, like his Dad, was also legally a 'stranger' or foreigner? Given that Toucher Guydon does not appear in the 1642 Parliamentary Attestation it seems probable that he also was a 'stranger' when his son Christopher was baptised in Harmondsworth in 1630. This would have placed Toucher into a lower level social position. Then in 1697 John and Elizabeth Guidon are 'touched' for the King's Evil, a doubtful privilege granted to those who were diseased as a result of malnutrition. This John Guidon was almost certainly a son or nephew of Christopher.

The Boyd's Index of Marriages records more than 40 people with the surnames of Dowton, Dowden and variants who were married in the London area in the period 1550 to 1700. It has not proved possible to place any of these people onto a family tree.

Considering now the archives for the west of London it is recorded that:

Thomas Dowden married Agnes Urlwin at West Drayton on 3rd April 1599,

Edward Dowden married Frances Wade at West Drayton on ? ? 1599,

John Dounton married Elizabeth Grove at Harefield on 16th July 1668, and

Richard Downton, son of Richard and Mary was baptised at Staines on 16th September 1678.

Clearly there were people named Dowden (and variants) living some 15 miles west of London during the 16th and 17th centuries. Recalling now that known forebear Thomas Dowton married Mary Guidon at West Drayton in 1725 it seems reasonable to deduce that this later Thomas was possibly a direct descendant of one of the 16th century Dowden's noted above.

In the latter part of the eighteenth century we find that Ralph Dowden, who clearly used his wits not always to his advantage, was frequently helped to survive by recourse to Poor Law funds. Also Ralph's wife Sarah died under tragic circumstances. Ralph's son William and his wife Mary clearly had a difficult time from a financial viewpoint, and then, as if to add insult to injury, William died in 1814 at about 44 years of age, leaving a widow and young family. In 1819 the Dowden family and most other local agricultural labourers had their access to the common land in their parish stolen from them by the local Inclosure Act. Life must have been desperately hard for those trying to survive during the 1820's. Was the impact of the Inclosure Act the reason for the action of James in his theft of poultry? We will never know the answer to this question. But we do know the end of the 'Uncle' James story. He was hanged in Australia shortly after having his back cut to ribbons after a sentence of fifty lashes. Great-grandfather Charles married late, lost several of his children while they were young, and had frequent recourse to Poor Law funds. Also, in mid-life, his wife died from the effects of severe burning. His life was

From the Bottom of the Pile

also very hard, and his death certificate says it all when it describes his cause of death as 'Worn Out'. Grandfather Joseph died at only 44 years of age, and grandmother Jessie died a month later, almost certainly an aftereffect of deep despair concerning her condition. The consequence of this on the early life of my father, and on certain of his emotional attitudes in later life, left much to be desired. Mum and Dad made the best they could out of what little they had, and for that they should be admired. But, as the writer knows only too well, theirs was not an easy life. Clearly most, if not indeed all, of my identified forebears lived out their lives in a position near the bottom of the social and financial scale.

But what of my generation? Obviously each of Mum and Dad's children are responsible for their own stories, but one thing is certain. My generation had opportunities unknown to our forebears and these, in various ways, we all used to our advantage. The stories of Mum and Dad's children, if ever written, cannot properly be given the title 'From the Bottom of the Pile', and in a significant measure we can thank our Mum and Dad for that.

Hopefully, at this point in the narrative the reader will permit me a paragraph of personal comments. At the time of writing it is as though the British people, and those who are English in particular, are being attacked and called to account on all sides in the media. There are a significant number of vociferous people in the Celtic parts of these islands who accuse 'The English' of all sorts of crimes. For example the English are guilty because of the impact of the Irish famine in the 1840's, guilty of the impact of the Highland clearances at about the same time, and so on. I'd like to know how my ancestors did anything during these periods of time that should cause me, on behalf of my forebears, to apologise to my Celtic cousins. Moving onto the world stage there are demands for the British to apologise for the slave trade, for the opium wars, for the empire, and so on. Again I would like to know how my ancestors had any impact on these matters such that I have any reason to apologise. There is no doubt that in the past the UK has been involved a number of events that we would not wish to condone today. But I suggest to the reader that in the whole sequence of events in my identified history, my forebears have been victims as opposed to perpetrators. I owe no-one an apology for perceived past misdeeds of my nation.

Moving on from the above rant, the following notes provide evidence for the noted aspects of the lives of my forebears. In the first two paragraphs below, relevant papers or microfiche copies have been seen by the writer, but no hard copies were made. All of the papers seen were copies of the original documents.

The earliest record seen by the writer was the Bishop's Transcript of 1630 indicating the baptism at St. Mary's Church Harmondsworth of Christopher Guydon, son of Toucher Guydon. The actual documents being perused at the time were microfiche copies of actual records. In practice all the investigative work concerning my forebears up to the death of my grandparents in 1907 was carried out during the early 1990's. This was before the development of the computer-aided search techniques available at the time of writing this appendix (2010). The

Appendix

1630 microfiche record, and indeed all other church-based records were seen as microfiche copies of the original documents, and these could not be photo-copied at the place and time they were investigated. It follows that the chapter Ancestral Documents does not include copies of church-based records.

The earliest original paper seen personally by the writer is a certificate, written at the time, concerning the 'Touching' at Harmondsworth on 23rd June 1697 of John and Elizabeth Guidon and others by King William III for 'The King's Evil'. This certificate is/was in the private possession of the current William Wild, descendant of many generations of William Wild's of Harmondsworth who, amongst other matters, gave Poor Law relief to many of my forebears. I am very grateful to William for his kindness in showing me both this certificate and other papers in his possession. The certificate was seen in William's private home and hence I do not have a copy of this paper. The first four 'record' papers in the Documents chapter are translations from the Latin originals of the Courts Baron, as they affected (only) my forebears for the years 1723, 1724 and 1726. Court Baron records are/were the property of the Lord of the Manor, and in the fullness of time a later generation may have no interest in preserving the records of events long ago. Such was the case concerning the Court Baron records of Harmondsworth. In (I think) the late 1980's a Mr. Aaron Janes 'rescued' some rolls of parchment from a junk shop, where they were due to be sold for uses such as coverings for lampshades. Mr Janes realised that he had bought documents of significant historical value, and hence he registered his holding with National Register of Archives. The documents were then bought by a Mr. Peter Lee for the West Middlesex Family History Society (WMFHS) and subsequently loaned to the London Metropolitan Archive (LMA). The 'purchase' was for the Court Baron records for Harmondsworth for the years 1717 to 1728. The WMFHS had the Latin original document translated into English and then made into a booklet. The first four papers are a copy of this translation.

The fifth paper, hand-written and dated 25th April 1726, is a photo-copy from the LMA of an 'original' scrap of paper found by my wife and I at the LMA in about 1995. We were searching through what can only be described as a random collection of papers from the Paget family when we came across this small piece of paper labelled 'Court Diuner' It is a summary paper of the financial aspects of Court Baron held on that day. This paper was found before we knew about the above 1717 to 1728 parchments find, and it was from this paper that it was realised that Mary Douton, wife of Thomas, was the daughter of John and Elizabeth Guidon. It was this paper that proved the Guidon link and hence enabled further tracing of the family tree from Thomas Douton, who died in 1747, back to the baptism of Christopher Guydon in year 1630. The certificate is a rental agreement dated 24th April 1738 enabling a John Guidon to become the tenant of a property.. This John was probably the brother of forebear Mary. Note at the foot of this document the spidery signature of Peter Walter, the Steward or legal officer of the Earl of Uxbridge, Lord of the Manor. This demonstrates the high degree of control exercised by the Earl in his Manor, in that even a tenancy agreement between the copyhold 'owner' of a cottage and a prospective tenant of this 'owner' had to be ratified by the Lord's Steward.

From the Bottom of the Pile

The 'Dowden' parts of the account of the Countess of Uxbridge Charity are self explanatory. It is however interesting to note the variation of spelling used. The noted John is Ralph's elder brother, the 'Wid' is Mary, John's widow. It was normal practice at that time to refer to a married lady as Dame Xxxx and then after the death of her husband as Widow Xxxx. The first name of these ladies was never used, at least by those in control in Harmondsworth.

In the essays concerning Ralph and William there are many noted instances in which my forebears received money from the Poor Law fund. The examples given have all been taken from the Vestry Minutes and not all have been copied. Examples of Vestry Minutes that have been copied are noted for 24th February and 10th March 1802. These are included because of the nature of the events they describe. On 24th February 1802 we see the operation of a health service in that Mary, wife of William, was in receipt of medical assistance that was being paid for by the Poor Law fund. On 10th March 1802 we see another example of a health service in that Mary is requesting that one of her sons should be inoculated against smallpox at the expense of the Poor Law fund. That Mary was wishing for her child to be inoculated with live smallpox virus is, to us, incredible. And when the Countess of Uxbridge brought the practice of inoculation with live smallpox virus to Harmondsworth in the early 1700's, she also was acting in terms of a health service for her manorial tenants. From the Church Fees document of 1813 one does not get the impression that the poor in desperate need of immediate clerical help, for matters such as the baptism of a newly born but sickly child, would be treated with kindness. But perhaps the facts on the ground at the time tell a different story. We will never know.

Coming now to 1799 James Dowden, it will never be known why he stole poultry in February 1820. The facts of the case can be downloaded by computer from the records of the Old Bailey, and that the reader is invited to do, but these records tell only what happened and not why. Following the arrival of James in Australia he was assigned to Longbottom Farm and the tale of the subsequent activities of James and others is taken from the nine Australian records made in the years 1822 to 1824. Of interest to the writer is the way in which the fate of James was used by others.

Two photographs of people are included in the Ancestral Documents chapter. The first is of James, brother of grandfather Joseph, and his young son also named James. This is the only known photograph of anyone in my grandfather's generation. The final photograph is that of my parents. It was taken in my back garden in about 1964.

Ancestral Documents

Manor of Harmondsworth in the county of Middlesex	Court Baron of the Right Honourable Henry, Earl of Uxbridge, lord of the aforesaid manor held the twenty-second day of April in the ninth year of the reign of George I, by the grace of God, King of Great Britain, France and Ireland and in the year of our Lord 1723, by Peter Walter, Esquire, Steward there.

        James Tillear   Christopher Blunt   Henry Youle
        John Atlee   William Wild   Philip Tillear
        William Syms   John White
                            Sworn

Garstner to Guydon	At this court it was found by the Homage that William Garstner, one of the customary tenants of this manor, outside the court, namely twenty-first day of April in the year of our Lord 1722, surrendered into the lord's hands by the hands and acceptance of William Syms and John White, two other customary tenants of the same manor All that one customary acre of land lying and being in a certain Shot called Shepards Pool Shot in the common field of the aforesaid manor called Harmondsworth Field, the land of Richard Combes being on the south side and the land of Robert Whittington being on the north side. To the use and behoof of the aforesaid John Guydon of Harmondsworth, his heirs and assigns forever. And now the aforesaid John came into this court and asked to be admitted to the premises. To whom the lord, by his aforesaid Steward, granted seisin thereof by the rod, to have and to hold the aforesaid premises with the appurtenances to the aforesaid John, his heirs and assigns, from the lord at the will of the lord according to the custom of the aforesaid manor by annual rent and services thence before owed and accustomed.
Fine £2..2s	He gave the lord by way of fine two pounds and two shillings and so was admitted thereupon as tenant and did fealty.

        Examined by me   P Walter
                                  Steward

From the Bottom of the Pile

Manor of Harmondsworth in the county of Middlesex	Court Baron of the Right Honourable Henry, Earl of Uxbridge, lord of the aforesaid manor held the twentieth day of April in the tenth year of the reign of George I, by the grace of God, King of Great Britain, France and Ireland and in the year of our Lord 1724, by Peter Walter, Esquire, there.

        Henry Youle   William Wild   John Atlee
        William Syms   Roger Urlewin   James Tillear
        John White   Christopher Blunt Robert Combes
                                Sworn

Blunt to Stone and his wife	At this court the Homage found that Christopher Blunt one of the customary tenants of this manor outside the court namely on twentieth day of April instant, surrendered into the lord's hands by the hands and acceptance of Henry Youle and John White, two other customary tenants of the same manor, All his cottage or customary tenement with the appurtenances situate and being in Moor Lane within the aforesaid manor now in the occupation of John Guydon To the use and behoof of Derick Stone and Mary now his wife for and during the term of their lives the remainder to the use of the heirs and assigns of the aforesaid Derick forever. And now the aforesaid Derick and Mary came into this court and asked to be admitted to the premises. To whom the lord, by his aforesaid Steward, granted seisin thereof by the rod, to have and to hold the aforesaid premises with the appurtenances to the aforesaid Derick and Mary in the manner and form aforesaid, from the lord at the will of the lord according to the custom of the aforesaid manor by annual rent and services thence before owed and accustomed.
Fine £7.	They gave the lord by way of fine seven pounds and so they were admitted thereupon as tenents and the aforesaid Derick did fealty.

        Examined by me   P Walter
                                    Steward

Manor of Harmondsworth the county of Middlesex	Court Baron of the Right Honourable Henry, Earl of Uxbridge, lord of the aforesaid manor held the twenty-fifth day of April in the twelfth year of the reign of George I, by the Grace of God, King of Great Britain, France and Ireland and in the year of our Lord 1726, by Peter Walter Esq, Steward there.

      James Tillear   Henry Youle   William Wild
      Christopher Blunt Richard Combes John White
      John Atlee
                          Sworn

Admission Tompkins according to the will of father	At this court it was found by the Homage that John Guidon one of the customary tenants of this manor outside the court namely, on the twelfth day of May last past surrendered into the lord's hands through the hands and acceptance of James Tillear and William Syms two other customary tenants of the said manor All his customary lands within the aforesaid manor to the use set out in his last Will And that the aforesaid John made his last Will in writing bearing date twelfth day of May aforesaid and by the same bequeathed in words to the effect following namely "I give and bequeath to my oldest daughter Elizabeth my one acre of copyhold Land lying in Harmondsworth field near Shephards Pool after the first crop after the date is taken of" as by the same Will he makes fully clear and apparent. And now the aforesaid Elizabeth, now the wife of Joseph Tomkins, came into this court and asked to be admitted to the premises. To whom the lord, by his aforesaid Steward, granted seisin therein by the rod, to have and to hold the aforesaid premises with the appurtenances to the aforesaid Elizabeth according to the aforesaid Will from the lord at the will of the lord according to the custom of the aforesaid manor by annual rent and services thence before owed and accustomed.
Fine £1..15s	She gave the lord by way of fine one pound fifteen shillings. And so was admitted thereupon as tenant etc.
Admission Downton according to the will of father	At this court it was found by the Homage that John Guidon one of the customary tenants of this manor outside the court namely, on the twelfth day of May last past surrendered into the lord's hands through the hands and acceptance of James Tillear and William Syms two other customary tenants of the said manor All his customary lands within the aforesaid manor to the use set out in his last Will And that the aforesaid John made his last Will in writing bearing date twelfth day of May aforesaid and by the same bequeathed in words to the effect following namely "I give and bequeath to my daughter Mary my one acre of copyhold land lying in Shepistone Field in a shot called little Acres after the first crop is taken off after the date hereof" as by the same Will makes fully clear and apparent. And now the aforesaid Mary, now the wife of Thomas Downton came into this court and asked to be admitted to the premises. To whom the lord, by his aforesaid Steward, has granted seisin thereof by the rod, to have and to hold the aforesaid premises with the appurtenances to the aforesaid Mary according to the aforesaid Will from the lord at the will of the lord according to the custom of the aforesaid manor by annual rent and services thence before owed and accustomed.

Fine £1..15s	She gave the lord by way of fine one pound fifteen shillings. And so was admitted thereupon as tenant etc.
Downton and wife to use of wife herself	At the aforesaid court sitting, the aforesaid Thomas Downton together with Mary his wife, in full and open court according to the custom (the same Mary being first examined alone and secretly by the Steward and thereupon consenting) surrendered into the lord's hands by the hands and acceptance of the aforesaid Steward All that aforesaid acre and third part of two and a half acres of which the aforesaid John Guydon died seized To the use and behoof of Mary for the term of her natural life and after the death of the aforesaid Mary then to the use of the aforesaid Thomas his heirs and assigns forever. And now the aforesaid Mary asked to be admitted to the premises. To whom the lord, by his aforesaid Steward, granted seisin thereof by the rod, to have and to hold the aforesaid premises with the appurtenances to the aforesaid Mary and Thomas in the manner and form aforesaid from the lord at the will of the lord according to the custom of the aforesaid manor by annual rent and services thence before owed and accustomed. And the aforesaid Mary was admitted thereupon as tenant etc.
Admission Guydon according to the Will of father	At this court it was found by the Homage that John Guidon one of the customary tenants of this manor outside the court namely, on the twelfth day of May last past surrendered into the lord's hands through the hands and acceptance of James Tillear and William Syms two other customary tenants of the said manor All his customary lands within the aforesaid manor use set out in his last Will And that the aforesaid John made his last Will in writing bearing date twelfth day of May aforesaid and by the same bequeathed in words to the effect following namely "I give and bequeath to my daughter Sarah my one half acre of Meadow ground lying in Wide Mead after the next Crop taken off" as by the same Will he made clear and apparent. And now the aforesaid Sarah, being an infant, by Elizabeth her mother and appointed guardian in court, asked to be admitted tenant to the premises. To whom the lord, by his aforesaid Steward, granted seisin thereof by the rod, to have and to hold the aforesaid premises with the appurtenances to the aforesaid Sarah according to the aforesaid Will from the lord at the will of the lord according to the custom of the aforesaid manor by annual rent and services thence before owed and accustomed.
Fine 16s	She gave the lord by way of fine sixteen shillings. And so was admitted thereupon as tenant etc.

                Examined by me   P Walter
                                           Steward

Manorium de Harmondsworth }   25. April 1726.

Elizabeth wife of Joseph Tombyns admitted to an acre of land on the Will of John Guidon her father   1:15:0

Mary wife of Thos. Downton to an acre on the Will of Do.   1:15:0

Sarah Guidon by her mother her guardian to half an acre on the Will of Do.   0:16:0

Thos. Downton to a 3 part of the 2 acres on the Surrender of his wife Mary   0:0:0

Wm. Blundell to a Messuage in Heathrow & 8 acres of land on ye Surr. of John Wilkins & Amy his wife   16:0:0

Wm. Fily a fine due last Court for admittance to the Estate late Mayleigh's   63:10:6

John Hornsby to a Cottage & acre & ½ by the death of John his father   6:10:0

Richard Combes Son to 17 acres of land on the death of his Mother   24:0:0

£ 114:6:6

Court Dinner 2:8:0

From the Bottom of the Pile

An Account of the Yearly Distribution of the Countess of Uxbridge Charity to the Poor of Harmondsworth. [DRO/123/083 at LMA]

[Front page] **Memorandum.**

The Rt. Honourable Elisabeth Countess Dowager of Uxbridge by Deed bearing Date 19th Feb 1747 did invest in John Atlee & John East of the Parish of Harmondsworth One Hundred Pounds in Old South Sea Annuities then carrying interest at the rate of 4 percent and therein directs that the said John Atlee & John East together with the Minister and Church-Wardens shall distribute the said interest annually upon New Year's Day to ten poor families not receiving Collection from the PSH & that an Account of such Distribution shall be entered into a Book kept 5 shillings being paid there out to the Trustee for Received the Money.

Jan 8 1758-9	Ralph Douden	5s 6d
Jan 12 1762	Ralph Dowden	5s 6d
Jan 12 1763	Ralph Dowden	5s 6d
Jan 12 1764	Ralf Dowden	4s 6d
Jan 12 1765	Ralf Dowden	5s 6d
Jan 8 1766	Ralf Dowden	5s 6d
Jan 8 1767	Ralph Dowden	5s 6d
Jan 11 1768	Ralph Dowden	6s
Jan 8 1770	John Dowden	5s 6d
Jan 8 1772	John Dowden	5s 6d
Jan 10 1773	John Dowden	5s 6d
Jan 8 1775	John Dowden	5s 0d
Jan 12 1778	Jno Dowdon	5s 6d
Jan 12 1779	Jno Dowden	5s 0d
Jan 12 1784	John Dowdon	6s
Jan 12 1786	Jno Dowden	5s 0d
Jan 12 1794	Wid Dowden	5s
Jan 12 1801	Wid Dowden	5s
Jan 12 1805	Wm Dowden	5s
Jan 12 1806	Wm Dowden	5s

Writer's note: This charity was discontinued in 1823 on the grounds of its being 'irregular'.

1802 — Feb'y 24th At a Vestry field at the Workhouse

A Bill of Mess'rs Pope Tothill & Chandler Surgeons for Certain Cures to Seabrooks Family at Stanwell amount £5-5-6 ordered to be paid

Dame Karman applied for payment for Nursing Will'm Dowdens wife in Laying in ordered to receive £1-1-0 from Mr Wild

Joseph Little applied for assistance for his wife in Case of Illness ordered 5th Stockmoney

Henry Darbon applied for assistance for his wife in Case of Lying in ordered to receive 10th Stockmoney

Dame Kendall applied for assistance for their family ordered to receive 7th Stockmoney

Agreed that the Following Persons be exam'd to their Settlements, Jos'a Darbon,
Wm Snowden
— Littlewood
John Peters
Rich'd Goodman
— Sale
Charles Hiller

James Tillyer
Rob't Sim oyer
William Jarvis
William Wild
Jos'h East
Wm M

Final name below:
Wm. Parrot

Ancestral Documents

1802 March 10th

At a Vestry held at the Sun Public House in the Parish of Harmondsworth Middx

Dame Hoar applied for assistance for her son ordered to receive four Shillings

William Dowden's wife applied for Relief for her Husband, order'd to receive as Mr Wild sees needful and desired to have one Child Inoculated

Joseph Little applied for assistance for his wife desired as Mr Wild sees Needfull

William Eagle's wife Applied for assistance for her Husband to receive as Mr Wild sees Needfull

Henry Darbon applied for assistance for his wife in lying in a Midwife to be paid £5 paid by Mr Wild

Robert Tomkins Constable's Bill 2/ paid by Mr

Thomas Hampton Glazier Bill for Mending the Windows at the Workhouse Amount 2-19-3 one Half to be paid by J Riddington other By the Overseer for the Parish the Windows now in good condition

a Bill of Thomas East for Mending the Window frames at the Workhouse to be paid By Mr Wild Amount — £-9-3

James Tillyer
William Jarvis
The Jarvis
W. Thurbin
Abel Hunt

Also:
Thos. Weekly
Wm. Parrot
William Taylor

St. Mary the Virgin Church - Harmondsworth

Table of Fees - 1813

Baptisms

	£.	s.	d.
In the church after divine service		1	0
If the church is opened on purpose		7	0
At home if illnefs render it necessary		10	6

Weddings

	£.	s.	d.
After banns including 1s-6d for publication of banns		6	6
With licence		10	6

Funerals

	£.	s.	d.
For a parishioner in the churchyard		2	0
For a vault in the church or churchyard	5	5	0
For a tomb rail in the church		15	0
For a stone over the grave	2	2	0
Undertakers pall		5	0
Opening a vault	1	1	0
Mortuary (for head of the family, male or female)		10	0
For a tablet in the church or against the church	2	2	0
For head - & footstones	1	11	6
For vaulted grave in the churchyard	2	2	0
For the desk service, when a vault is opened in the church		4	0

No. Every article is doubled for a non-parishioner, to which is added 2s-0d. £1-1s-0d for opening the ground in the churchyard.

Frederick Tomkins Vicar.

Colonial Secretary's Correspondence   1788 - 1825

DOWDEN, James

1822 Jan 28   Attached to Longbottom. On return of proceedings of the Bench of Magistrates, Parramatta

---

(Fiche 3297; X643 p.2b)

Return of Proceedings taken at the Magistrates Court, Parramatta for the Quarter ending March 31st, 1822

Date	Jan 28, 1822
Present	Henry G Douglas Esq
Names	James Dowden
Free or Bond	Bond
If Bond, by what ship?	Bearing 2
Nature of Offence	Neglect of work and Insolence to his Overseer
Sentence	50 lashes and to be returned to his gang
Remissions	Nil
Remarks	Attached to Longbottom

1822 Sydney Gazette   (published weekly each Friday)

The following appeared in a column headed Principal Superintendent's Office – and in the editions of Feb 15th, Feb 22nd, and Mar 22nd, James was mentioned amongst many others as below.

> *The Undermentioned Prisoners, having absented themselves from their respective employment and some of them at large with false Certificates, all Constables and others are herby required to use their utmost exertions in apprehending and lodging them in Custody.*
>
> ....   *Geo King, Wm King, Jas Dowder, Moses Harper & James Riley from Longbottom Farm,* ....

Same paper, under the same heading, and again amongst many others, James continued to appear, as follows, in the editions of March 29th, April 5th, April 12th, April 19th, April 26th, May 3rd and May 10th. –

> *James Dowton, arrived per Hebe; 20 years old, native of Middlesex, 5'8½" high, hazel eyes, black hair, dark ruddy complextion; and belonged to Longbottom Farm.*

Sydney Gazette   Criminal Court   Friday June 14th 1822

> *Wednesday. James Dowden, aged 22 was indicted for committing a burglary on 21st Feb last in the Dwelling House of John Sunderland at the Dog Traps near the Parramatta Road. And also with another burglary in the house of Thomas Salmon the prisoner pleaded Guilty. Remanded.*

Ancestral Documents

Colonial Secretary's Correspondence   **1788 - 1825**

DOWDEN, James Per "Hebe", 1820 bushranger

1822 Jun 1 - 18   Sentenced to death. In reports of prisoners tried at Court of Criminal Jurisdiction

---

(Reel 6023; X820 p.53)

Name	James Dowden
Charges	Charged with burglariously breaking and entering the Dwelling House of John Sunderland at the Dog Traps near Parramatta and feloniously stealing therefrom certain Goods.
	Also charged with robbing Thomas Salmon on the Kings Highway near the South Creek and stealing certain goods from the person.
Judgement	Guilty
Sentence	Death
Remarks	Nil

Colonial Secretary's Correspondence   1788 - 1825

DOWDEN, James   Per "Hebe", 1820   bushranger

1822 Jul 3,29   Captured on information supplied by John Hinns; appears as Dowton.

(Reel 6055; 4/1761 pp.3)

Shanes Park South Creek

July 3rd, 1822

Sir,   I beg most respectfully to call to your recollection the conversation I had with you respecting the man who had given me the information and was the means of the apprehension of Dowton the Bush Ranger, and of my promise then, if his information was correct, that I would use my influence with His Excellency to have something done for him, On Dowton being taken and on my sensing for him to know what he expected for the service done, he very modestly replied that if His Excellency would Grant him a Ticket of Leave he would feel perfectly content.

I have therefore to beg you to kindly solicit His Excellency to grant him that indulgence on account of my promise to him.

The man bears a good character, his name is John Hinnes, he came in the 1st Baring, Lamb Master.

I remain with much respect, Sir
Your most obedient H^{m} S^{erv}
J Harris

PS   I am just informed that Hopkins, and other Bush Rangers are at the Cow Pastures. They shall be sent after immediately.

Ancestral Documents

Colonial Secretary's Correspondence   **1788 - 1825**

DOWDEN, James Per "Hebe", 1820 bushranger

1822 Jul 5   Executed

(Reel 6070; 4/1265 p.39)   1788-1825   **Death Warrant**

Date	1st July 1822
Name	James Dowden
Where Tried	Sydney
When	Sessions commencing 1-18 June 1822 and 18th of same month
Offence	Felony
Date of Execution	5th July 1822

Colonial Secretary's Correspondence   1788 - 1825

DOWDEN, James   Per "Hebe", 1820 bushranger

1822 Jul 3,29   Captured on information supplied by John Hinns; appears as Dowton.

(Reel 6055; 4/1761 p.70)

Shanes Park South Creek

July 29th, 1822

May it please your Excellency

    The bearer Wm Hinns through whose information Dowton the Bush Ranger was taken, was promised by me should his assertion be correct and crowned with success, that I would use my influence with Your Excellency to have something done for him. But on the contrary if he gave me false intelligence, that I would punish him. He did give me the necessary clue and the Constables were successful. On asking him what he expected to be done for him, he replied that the Ticket of Leave would be as much as he expected.

    On making this known to Major Goulburn the major desired that I would inform Hinns That if he would come down to Sydney any Tuesday that he would speak to Your Excellency and procure him a Ticket as required. I further beg to assure you that the bearer is the man, and that he has had no participation in any reward concerning the apprehension of said Dowton. And further that he is a man of good character That he was the Government Servant to Mr Minchin but is now a shepherd with Major Druitt.

    I have the honour to remain with the greatest respect and esteem

        Your Excellency's most obedient and humble servant

            J Harris

Colonial Secretary's Correspondence 1788 - 1825

DOWDEN, James Per "Hebe", 1820 bushranger

1822 Nov Referred to in petition of John Slater for mitigation of sentence

---

(Fiche 3226; 4/1867 p.76)

To His Excellency, Major General Sir Thomas Brisbane K.C.B Captain General, Governor and Commander in Chief.

The Humble Petition of John Slater Respectfully Sheweth –

That Petitioner arrived in this Colony per ship Larkins (Wilkinson Master) in the year 1817 under Sentence of Exile for Life and was assigned to John Harris Esquire whose service he remained in until the month of March last when he was appointed a Constable.

Petitioner had now the benefit of a Ticket of Leave received from the Colonial Secretary on the arrival of his wife and Three Children in the month of January last as Free Subjects. He was at the apprehending of James Dowder a noted Bush Ranger, where he used every exertion in his power to effect the same.

Petitioner had over all conducted himself with Honesty and Propriety and most humbly begs to Solicit Your Excellency may be pleased to take the circumstances of his case into your humane consideration and graciously design to Grant him a Conditional Pardon.

For which Petitioner will as in duty bound ever pray.

John Slater

NSW
November 1822

(Recommended)

Colonial Secretary's Correspondence   **1788 - 1825**

DOWDEN, James Per "Hebe", 1820 bushranger

1824 Jan 28 Re apprehension of; appears as Dawden

(Film 6061; 4/1778 p. 64) (Date on film is 1824, Aug 23)

The Humble Petition of Stephen Curran sheweth -

    That the Petitioner came to this Colony by the ship Baring (??) under Sentence of Exile for Fourteen Years has been the whole of the time with Government – acting as Constable and Scourger.

    That in August 1822 in consequence of Petitioner being active in apprehending James Dawden, a notorious Bushranger (who has been since executed) Your Excellency be pleased to extend to him a Conditional Pardon.

    That Petitioner being now out of Employ and in consequence of his Active Service rendered to the Crown makes him obnoxious to the public in general, and precludes him obtaining any kind of Labour.

    (Several more paragraphs followed, but absolutely nothing to do with James)

Final comment at end of page

Directed to apply to the Chief Engineer as the only office likely to employ him.

Colonial Secretary's Correspondence   1788 - 1825

DOWDEN, James Per "Hebe", 1820 bushranger

1824   Memorial of Catherine Slater

(Fiche 3109; 4/1839A p.741)

To His Excellency Sir Thomas Brisbane KCB Captain General, Governor and Commander in Chief (General) over H.M Territory of New South Wales and its Dependencies.

The Memorial of Catherine Slater most Humbly Sheweth -

That Your Excellency's Humble Memorialist came Free to this Colony by the ship "Providence" in 1822 for the purpose of ……….. being with and …..……. the grief of her husband John Slater a Constable in the District of Melville and possessed of a Ticket of Leave.

That Your Excellency's Memorialiste has a family of Four (4) Children.

That Your Excellency's Memorialist's Husband was one of the party who at the hazard of their lives took into Custody a Bush Ranger named James Dowdell who was convicted and executed for a Capital Crime.

Your Excellency's Memorialiste therefore …….. humbly prays that Your Excellency will be pleased to take this familys case into Your Excellency's humane consideration by extending the ………….. benevolence of Your Excellency's condescending to bestow on her the Indulgence of a Grant of Land.

Your Excellency's most Humble Memorialiste as in duty bound, will humbly Pray.

Added at end

(The above statement is perfectly correct.)

In reply to your memorial requesting the Indulgence of a Grant of Land I am directed to acquaint you that as soon as you obtain any ……….. land will be allowed to you on the terms of an T of O.

FROM THE BOTTOM OF THE PILE

St. Mary's Church, Harmondsworth

The interior of Harmondsworth Great Barn.

Ancestral Documents

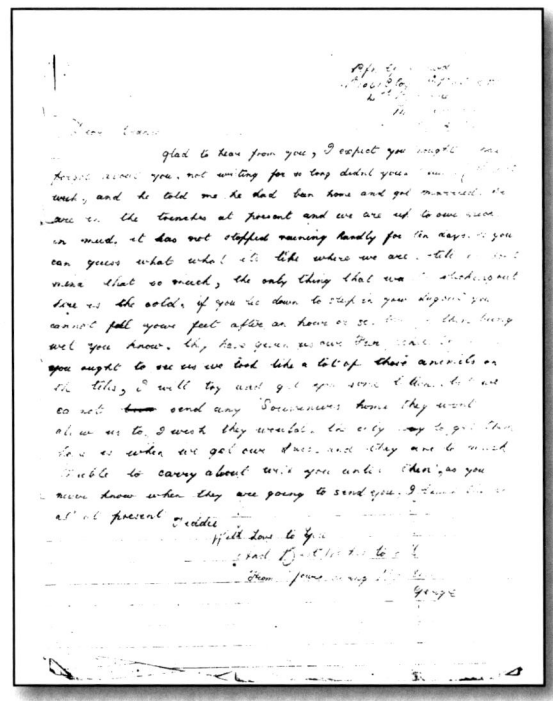

Rfn G. Dowden
No. 1061 C Coy 7th Batt KRR
41st Brigade
14th Division
B.E.F.

Dear Teddie

glad to hear from you, I expect you thought I had forgot about you, not writing for so long didnt you, I saw Mick last week, and he told me he had been home and got married, We are in the trenches at present and we are up to our necks in mud, it has not stopped raining hardly for ten days so you can guess what its like where we are, still we don't mind that so much, the only thing that wants sticking out here is the cold, if you lie down to sleep in your dugout you cannot feel your feet after an hour or so, through them being wet you know, they have given us our Fur jackets this with you ought to see us we look like a lot of those animals on the tiles, I will try to get some buttons, but we cannot send any Souvenirs home they wont allow us to, I wish they would, the only way to get them home is when we get our Pass and they are to much trouble to carry about with you until then, as you never know when they are going to send you, I think this is all at present
Teddie
With Love to You
And Best Wishes to all
From Your Loving Brother
George

From the Bottom of the Pile

J. Dowden, Chimney Sweep, with his son, in Fulham Park Gardens, 1893

Mum and Dad, 1964

Family Trees

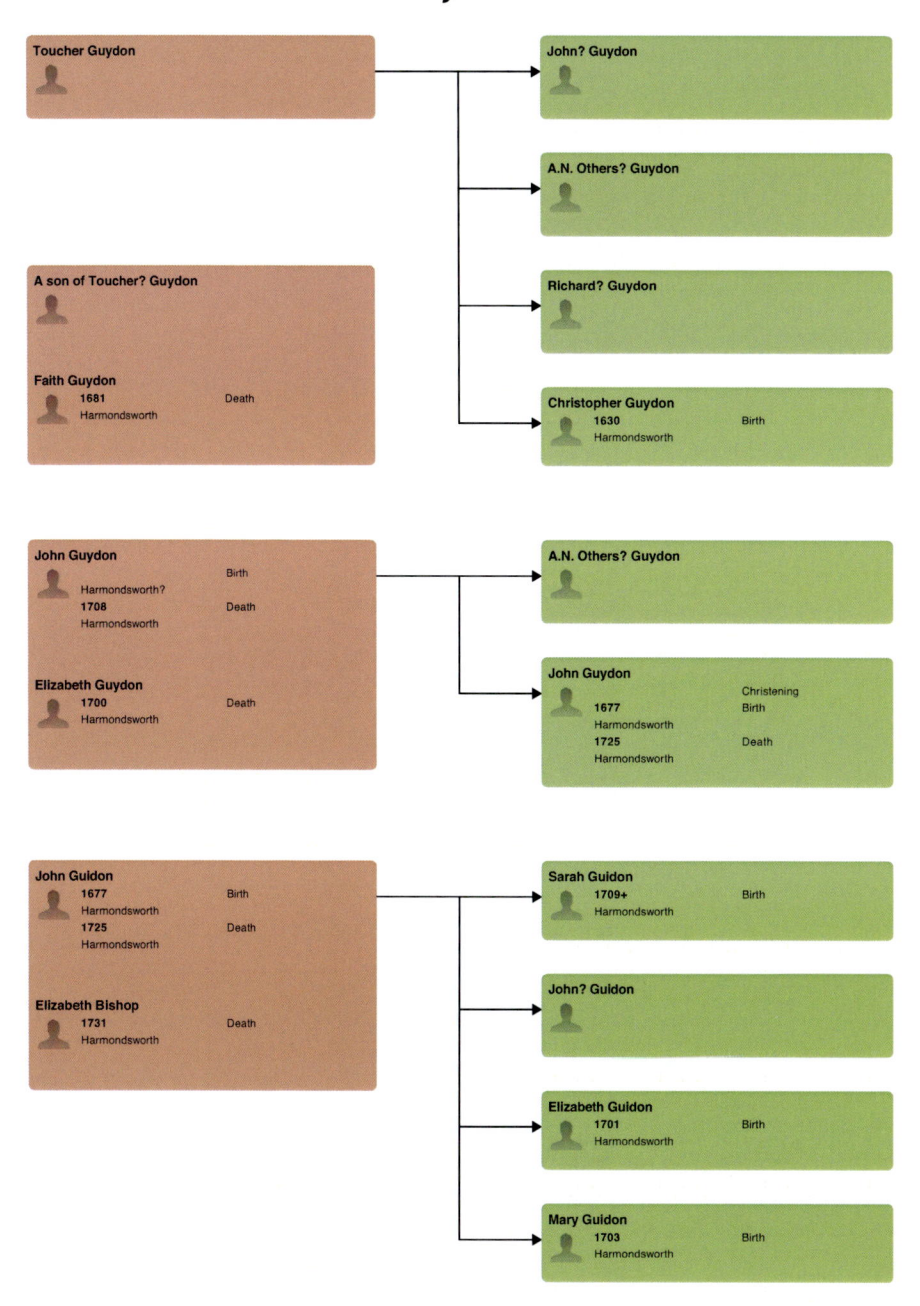

Toucher Guydon

A son of Toucher? Guydon

Faith Guydon
1681 — Death
Harmondsworth

John Guydon
Harmondsworth? — Birth
1708 — Death
Harmondsworth

Elizabeth Guydon
1700 — Death
Harmondsworth

John Guidon
1677 — Birth
Harmondsworth
1725 — Death
Harmondsworth

Elizabeth Bishop
1731 — Death
Harmondsworth

John? Guydon

A.N. Others? Guydon

Richard? Guydon

Christopher Guydon
1630 — Birth
Harmondsworth

A.N. Others? Guydon

John Guydon
1677 — Christening
Harmondsworth — Birth
1725 — Death
Harmondsworth

Sarah Guidon
1709+ — Birth
Harmondsworth

John? Guidon

Elizabeth Guidon
1701 — Birth
Harmondsworth

Mary Guidon
1703 — Birth
Harmondsworth

111

From the Bottom of the Pile

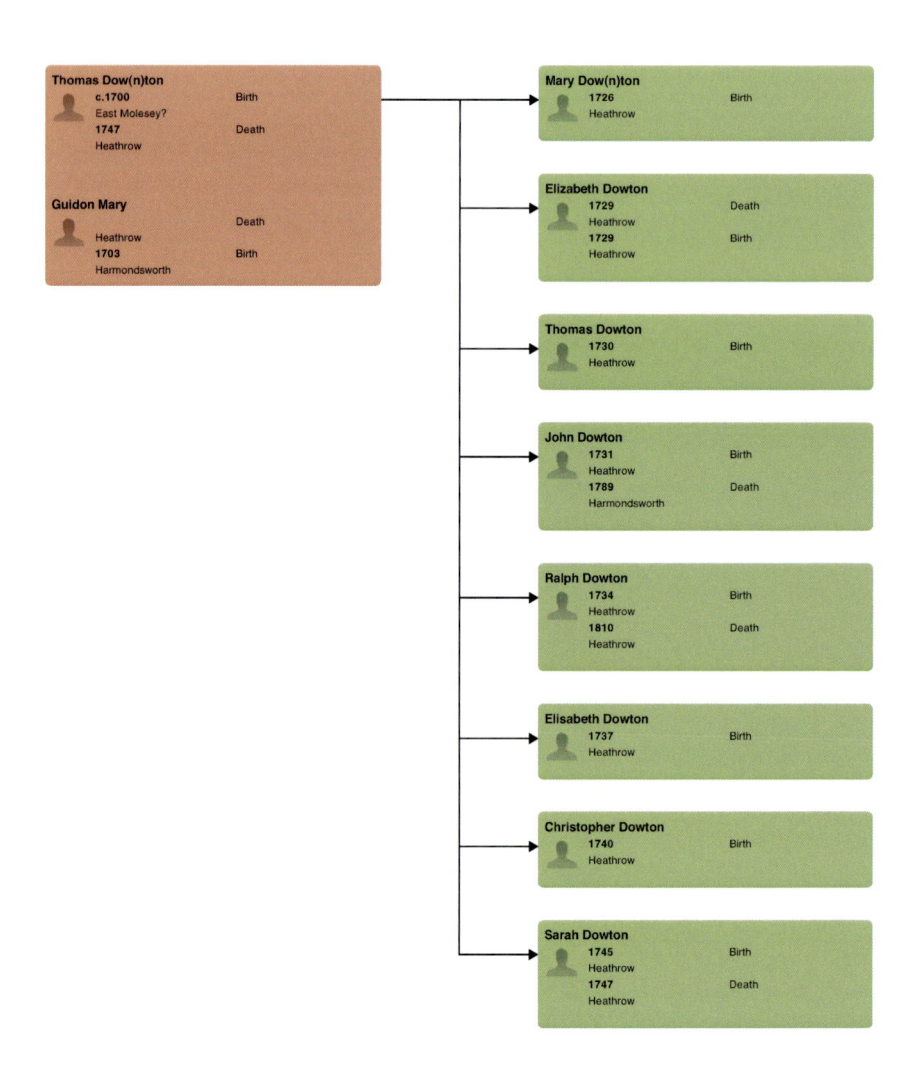

Thomas Dow(n)ton
- c.1700 — Birth
- East Molesey?
- 1747 — Death
- Heathrow

Guidon Mary
- Heathrow — Death
- 1703 — Birth
- Harmondsworth

Mary Dow(n)ton
- 1726 — Birth
- Heathrow

Elizabeth Dowton
- 1729 — Death
- Heathrow
- 1729 — Birth
- Heathrow

Thomas Dowton
- 1730 — Birth
- Heathrow

John Dowton
- 1731 — Birth
- Heathrow
- 1789 — Death
- Harmondsworth

Ralph Dowton
- 1734 — Birth
- Heathrow
- 1810 — Death
- Heathrow

Elisabeth Dowton
- 1737 — Birth
- Heathrow

Christopher Dowton
- 1740 — Birth
- Heathrow

Sarah Dowton
- 1745 — Birth
- Heathrow
- 1747 — Death
- Heathrow

Family Trees

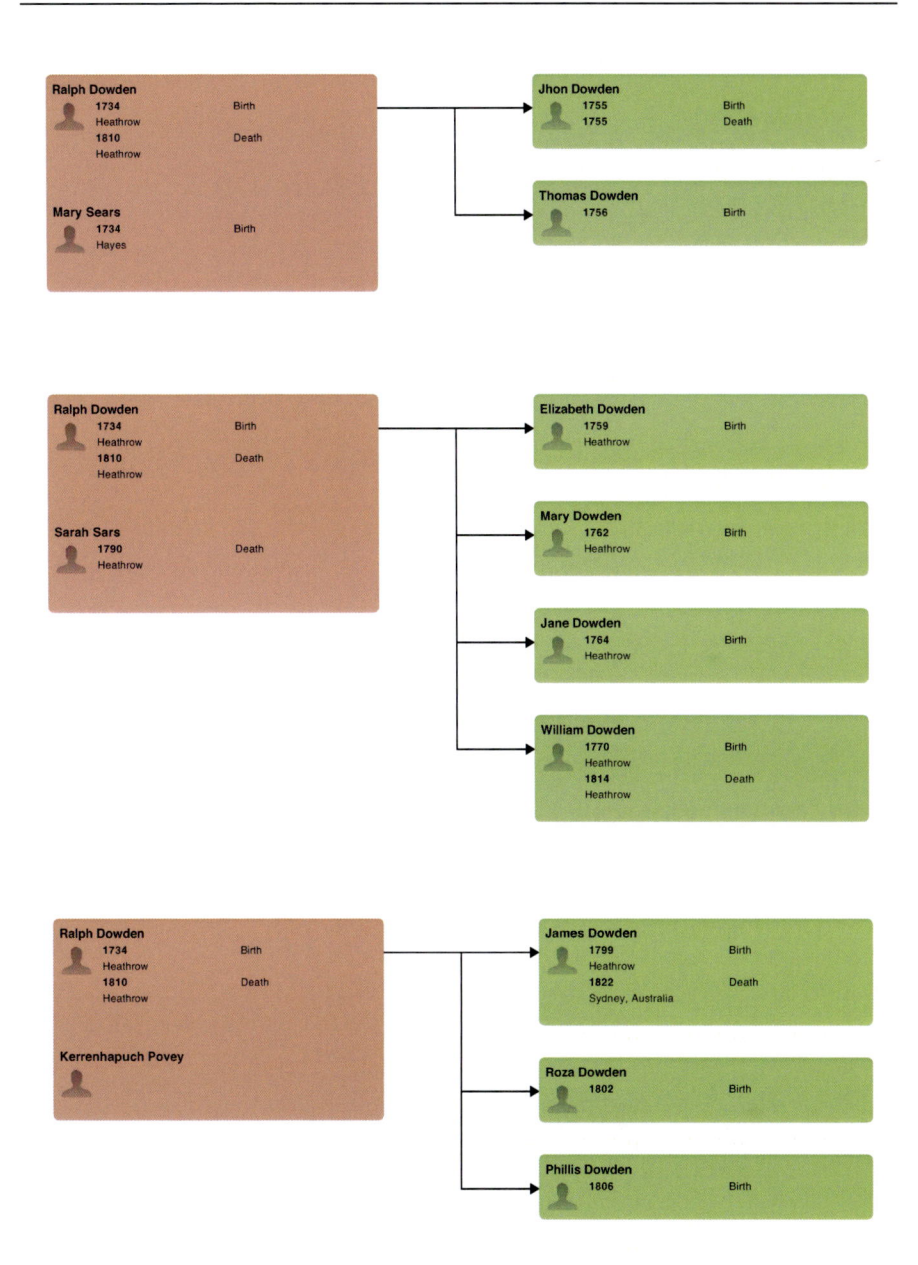

Ralph Dowden
- 1734 Heathrow — Birth
- 1810 Heathrow — Death

Mary Sears
- 1734 Hayes — Birth

→ **Jhon Dowden**
- 1755 — Birth
- 1755 — Death

→ **Thomas Dowden**
- 1756 — Birth

Ralph Dowden
- 1734 Heathrow — Birth
- 1810 Heathrow — Death

Sarah Sars
- 1790 Heathrow — Death

→ **Elizabeth Dowden**
- 1759 Heathrow — Birth

→ **Mary Dowden**
- 1762 Heathrow — Birth

→ **Jane Dowden**
- 1764 Heathrow — Birth

→ **William Dowden**
- 1770 Heathrow — Birth
- 1814 Heathrow — Death

Ralph Dowden
- 1734 Heathrow — Birth
- 1810 Heathrow — Death

Kerrenhapuch Povey

→ **James Dowden**
- 1799 Heathrow — Birth
- 1822 Sydney, Australia — Death

→ **Roza Dowden**
- 1802 — Birth

→ **Phillis Dowden**
- 1806 — Birth

From the Bottom of the Pile

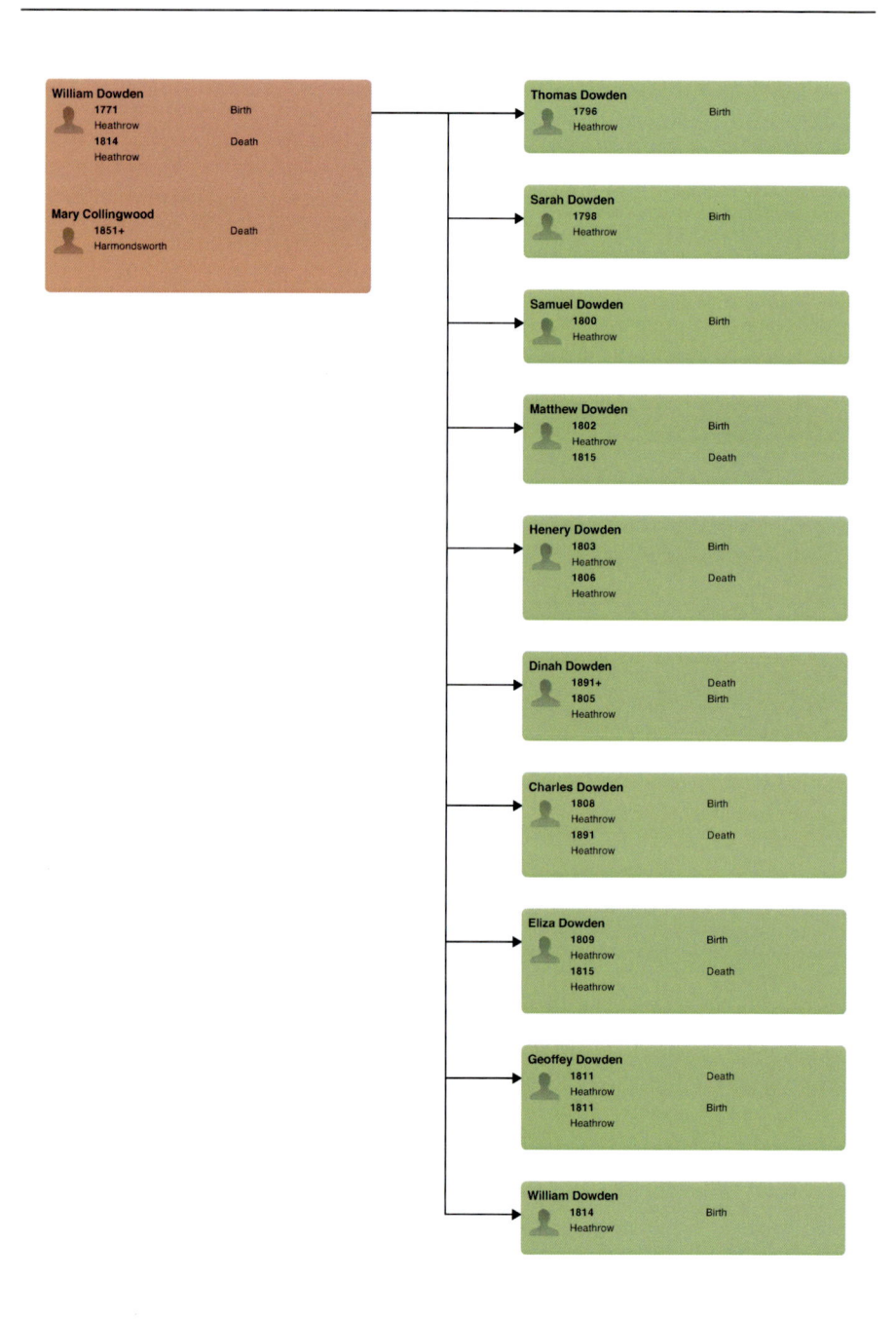

William Dowden
- 1771 Birth — Heathrow
- 1814 Death — Heathrow

Mary Collingwood
- 1851+ Death — Harmondsworth

Thomas Dowden
- 1796 Birth — Heathrow

Sarah Dowden
- 1798 Birth — Heathrow

Samuel Dowden
- 1800 Birth — Heathrow

Matthew Dowden
- 1802 Birth — Heathrow
- 1815 Death

Henery Dowden
- 1803 Birth — Heathrow
- 1806 Death — Heathrow

Dinah Dowden
- 1891+ Death
- 1805 Birth — Heathrow

Charles Dowden
- 1808 Birth — Heathrow
- 1891 Death — Heathrow

Eliza Dowden
- 1809 Birth — Heathrow
- 1815 Death — Heathrow

Geoffey Dowden
- 1811 Death — Heathrow
- 1811 Birth — Heathrow

William Dowden
- 1814 Birth — Heathrow

Family Trees

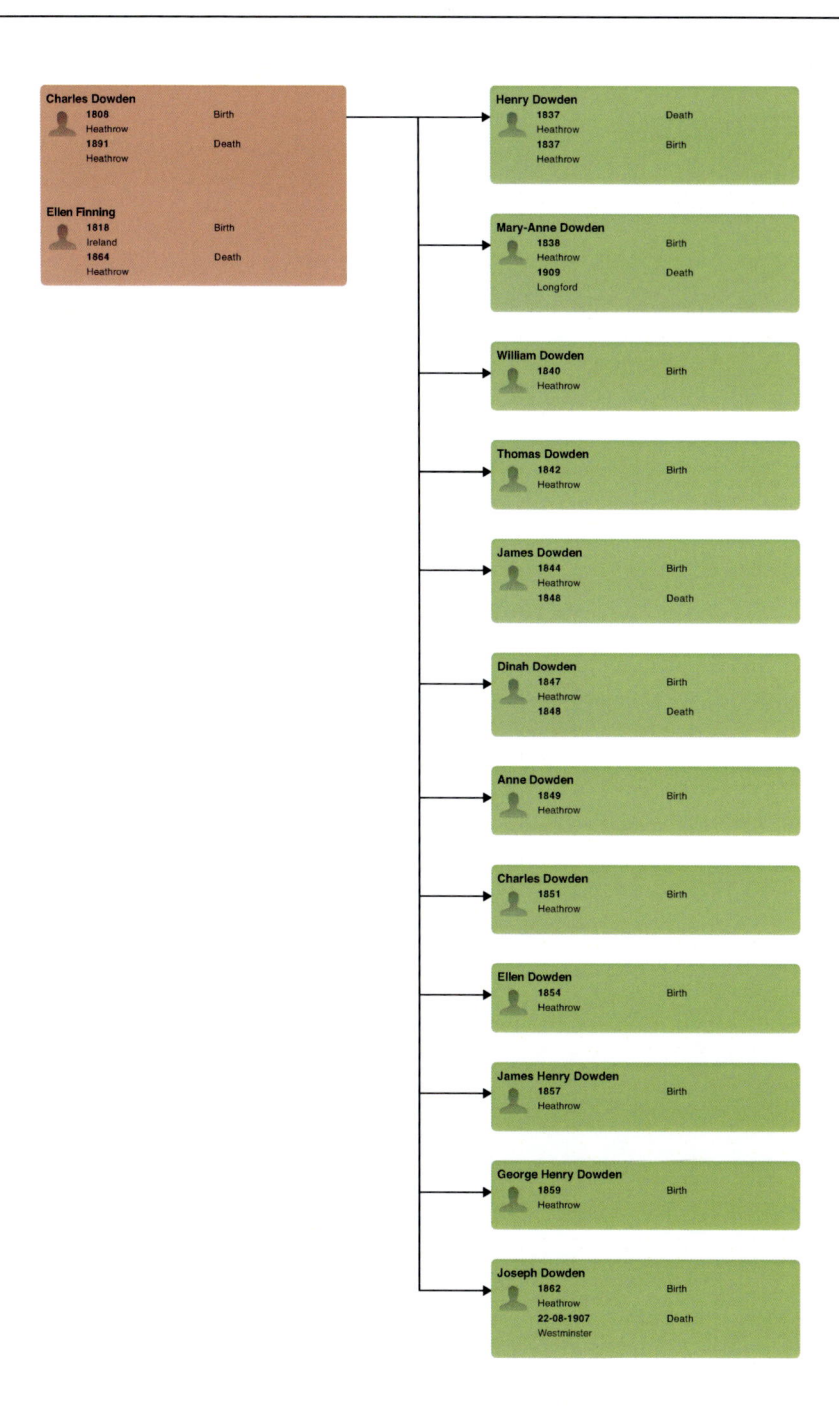

Charles Dowden
- 1808 Heathrow — Birth
- 1891 Heathrow — Death

Ellen Finning
- 1818 Ireland — Birth
- 1864 Heathrow — Death

Henry Dowden
- 1837 Heathrow — Death
- 1837 Heathrow — Birth

Mary-Anne Dowden
- 1838 Heathrow — Birth
- 1909 Longford — Death

William Dowden
- 1840 Heathrow — Birth

Thomas Dowden
- 1842 Heathrow — Birth

James Dowden
- 1844 Heathrow — Birth
- 1848 — Death

Dinah Dowden
- 1847 Heathrow — Birth
- 1848 — Death

Anne Dowden
- 1849 Heathrow — Birth

Charles Dowden
- 1851 Heathrow — Birth

Ellen Dowden
- 1854 Heathrow — Birth

James Henry Dowden
- 1857 Heathrow — Birth

George Henry Dowden
- 1859 Heathrow — Birth

Joseph Dowden
- 1862 Heathrow — Birth
- 22-08-1907 Westminster — Death

From the Bottom of the Pile

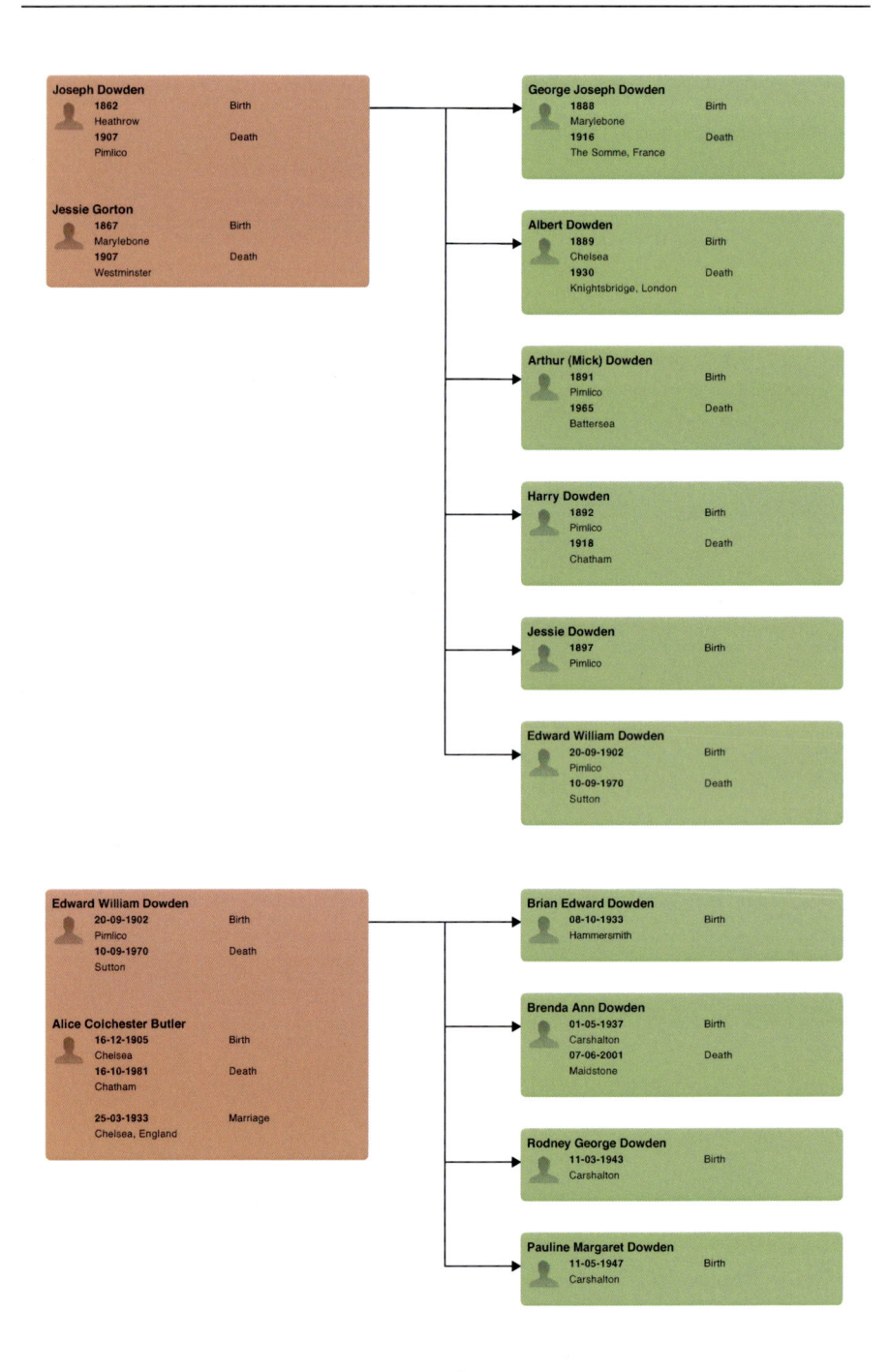

Joseph Dowden
1862 — Birth
Heathrow
1907 — Death
Pimlico

Jessie Gorton
1867 — Birth
Marylebone
1907 — Death
Westminster

George Joseph Dowden
1888 — Birth
Marylebone
1916 — Death
The Somme, France

Albert Dowden
1889 — Birth
Chelsea
1930 — Death
Knightsbridge, London

Arthur (Mick) Dowden
1891 — Birth
Pimlico
1965 — Death
Battersea

Harry Dowden
1892 — Birth
Pimlico
1918 — Death
Chatham

Jessie Dowden
1897 — Birth
Pimlico

Edward William Dowden
20-09-1902 — Birth
Pimlico
10-09-1970 — Death
Sutton

Edward William Dowden
20-09-1902 — Birth
Pimlico
10-09-1970 — Death
Sutton

Alice Colchester Butler
16-12-1905 — Birth
Chelsea
16-10-1981 — Death
Chatham

25-03-1933 — Marriage
Chelsea, England

Brian Edward Dowden
08-10-1933 — Birth
Hammersmith

Brenda Ann Dowden
01-05-1937 — Birth
Carshalton
07-06-2001 — Death
Maidstone

Rodney George Dowden
11-03-1943 — Birth
Carshalton

Pauline Margaret Dowden
11-05-1947 — Birth
Carshalton